GLOBETROTTER™

Travel Guide

MADAGASCAR

Derek Schuurman and
Nivo Ravelojaona

NEW HOLLAND

★★★ Highly recommended
★★ Recommended
★ See if you can

Fourth edition published in 2013
by New Holland Publishers (UK) Ltd
London • Cape Town • Sydney • Auckland
10 9 8 7 6 5 4 3 2 1
website: www.newhollandpublishers.com

Garfield House, 86 Edgware Road
London W2 2EA, United Kingdom

Wembley Square, First Floor, Solan Road
Cape Town 8001, South Africa

Unit 1, 66 Gibbes Street, Chatswood
NSW 2067, Australia

218 Lake Road, Northcote
Auckland, New Zealand

Distributed in the USA by
The Globe Pequot Press, Connecticut

Keep us Current
Information in travel guides is apt to change, which is why we regularly update our guides. We'd be grateful to receive feedback if you've noted something we should include in our updates. If you have new information, please share it with us by writing to the Publishing Manager, Globetrotter, at the office nearest to you (addresses on this page). The most significant contribution to each new edition will receive a free copy of the updated guide.

ISBN 978 1 78009 423 6

Publishing Manager: Thea Grobbelaar
DTP Cartographic Manager: Genené Hart
Editors: Thea Grobbelaar, Claudia dos Santos, Carla Redelinghuys, Donald Reid, Susannah Coucher
Picture Researchers: Shavonne Govender, Sonya Cupido
Design and DTP: Nicole Bannister, Gillian Black, Sonya Cupido
Cartographers: Tracey-Lee Fredericks, Reneé Spocter, Genené Hart, Éloïse Moss
Reproduction by Hirt & Carter (Pty) Ltd, Cape Town.
Printed and bound by Craft Print International Ltd, Singapore

Acknowledgments:
Thanks to (in alphabetical order): Franco Andreone, Toky Andrianamoro, Chantal Andríantseheno, Daniel Austin, Rita Bachmann, Olivier Behra, Gillian Black, Jim Bond, Corinna Botoulas, Hilary Bradt, Marius Burger, Rhett Butler, Paddy Bush, Christiane Chabaud, Gerald Cubitt, Adrian Deneys, Cedric de Foucault, Judith De Witt and Daniel Peters De Witt, Rachel Dobb, Rainer Dolch, Brian Donaldson, Agnes Rougeot and all at Rainbow Tours UK, Lee Durrell, Barry Ferguson, Duncan Guy, Alison Holman, Alison Jolly, Olivier Langrand, Richard Lewis, Lyn Mair, Eric Mathieu, Rob Morley, Erik Patel, Seraphine Tierney Ramanantsoa, Tsiry Rasetriarivony, Lalaina Ramaroson, the Ravelojaona family, Don Reid, Donald M Reid, Monique Rodrigues, Roger Safford (BirdLife International), Ian Sinclair, Lucienne Wilme, Porter P Lowry, Peter Raven and all at Missouri Botanical Gardens, Patricia Wright, Glyn Young, and the Za Tours team in Antananarivo.

Photographic Credits:
Franco Andreoni: page 15; **Danita Delimont Stock/awl-images.com:** cover; **Paul Biseth:** page 78, 83; **Corinna Botoulas:** pages 17, 21, 26, 30, 35, 81; **Marius Burger:** page 74, 105; **Constance Lodge Tsarabanjina:** page 98; **Gerald Cubitt:** title page, pages 4, 7, 9–13, 18–20, 24, 36, 39–42, 44, 46, 50, 53, 56, 57, 59, 61–64, 66, 70, 79–80, 86, 89–94, 96–98, 102, 111–115, 118; **Ian Davidson:** page 108; **Adrian Deneys:** pages 6, 58, 73, 83, 109; **Horst Gossler:** pages 33, 34, 98; **Duncan Guy:** page 32; **David Hardy:** page 29; **Olivier Langrand:** page 117; **Eric Mathieu:** page 119; **Boogie Pilgrim:** pages 55, 102, 111; **Catherine Price:** page 104; **Princesse Bora Lodge:** pages 112, 113; **David Rogers:** page 75, 76; **Derek Schuurman:** pages 14, 28, 77, 107; **Richard Stott:** page 80; **Ariadne van Zandbergen/Images of Africa:** page 65; **Franz Weber:** pages 116, 117.

Front Cover: *The Crested Coua is endemic to Madagascar.*
Title Page: *View of the patchwork quilt-like effect created by rice paddies around Antananarivo (Tana).*

CONTENTS

1. Introducing Madagascar 5
The Land 6
History in Brief 15
Government and Economy 24
The People 29

2. Antananarivo and the Highlands 37
Antananarivo 38
Around Antananarivo 40
Antsirabe to Fianarantsoa 41
Ranomafana National Park 43
Fianarantsoa to Ihosy 44

3. Southern Madagascar 51
Tuléar and Surrounds 52
Fort Dauphin (Tôlañaro) and Surrounds 59
Berenty Private Reserve 62
Andohahela National Park 65
Ifotaka Community Forest 66

4. Western Madagascar 71
Mahajanga 71
Anjajavy 75
Morondava and Surrounds 77
South of Morondava 83

5. Northern Madagascar 87
Diégo Suarez (Antsirañana) 88
Montagne d'Ambre National Park 89
Ankarana Special Reserve 91
The Nosy Bé Archipelago 93

6. Eastern Madagascar 103
Antananarivo to Tamatave 103
Tamatave and Surrounds 111
Ste Marie Island (Nosy Boraha) 112
Maroantsetra and the Masoala Peninsula 114
Masoala National Park 116
Sambava 118
Marojejy National Park 118

Travel Tips 122

Index 127

1 Introducing Madagascar

The world's fourth largest island after Greenland, New Guinea and Borneo, Madagascar is a land of dramatic contrasts and one which has long been renowned for its exceptionally diverse landscapes, flora and fauna, as well as the intriguing culture of its people, the world's only Afro-Asian nation. In the 16 years since the first edition of this guide was published, the country has undergone enormous change. This includes significant infrastructural improvements to cater for the growing international interest in the island as a tourist destination. There is something in Madagascar for everyone: nature lovers are inevitably enchanted by the compelling uniqueness of its fauna and its incomparably diverse flora. Active travellers can partake in an extensive range of outdoor adventure activities, while those after rest and relaxation can luxuriate at the small but growing number of quality seaside establishments.

Often referred to as the **Great Red Island** because of its red clay soils, Madagascar splintered off from the super-continent Gondwana between 120 and 165 million years ago, creating a geographic isolation from Africa and India which facilitated the gentle evolution of its animals and plants in a protective environment, largely free from predators. The result was a peculiar assemblage of life forms, including several species of pygmy hippopotamus, lemurs up to the size of a female gorilla, and various elephant birds, one of which stood 3m (10ft) and weighed 450–500kg (approximately 1000 lb).

Humans, on the other hand, probably arrived in Madagascar only about 2000 years ago, by means of out-

Top Attractions

*** **Unique wildlife and flora:** nature's living laboratory of evolution attracts more than 70% of visitors.
*** **Spectacular scenery:** explore mountains, rainforests, rivers and reefs.
*** **Beaches:** luxuriate in style on tropical offshore isles such as Nosy Tsarabanjina and Ste Marie, or at Anjajavy.
*** **Malagasy culture:** enjoy learning about the fascinating culture of the Malagasy people.

◀ *Opposite: Female black lemur. This species can easily be seen on Nosy Komba and along the Lokobe nature trail, Nosy Bé. Males are jet black.*

Best Beaches

The following are particularly inviting:
- Nosy Tsarabanjina; Manafiafy and Baobab Beach for fine, white sand beaches and dazzling coral reefs.
- Ste Marie's secluded, palm-fringed coves with whale-watching in season.
- Anjajavy for sunny beaches, quality accommodation and wildlife in baobab forests.

rigger canoes from Southeast Asia and Africa. Separated into many tribes, sub-tribes and innumerable clans, the approximately 22 million Malagasy are united by language and an endlessly intriguing culture.

Prospective visitors should bear in mind that while there are all the necessary ingredients for memorable getaways, Madagascar is still a poor country with a difficult geography and the tourist infrastructure remains modest. But it is this very lack of infrastructure that beckons some: substantial parts of the island are still poorly explored by westerners at time of writing, and in terms of natural history, few places are as fascinating.

THE LAND

Highlands and Lowlands

Much of Madagascar consists of a **Cambrian** and **pre-Cambrian** central plateau which once comprised part of the supercontinent Gondwana. In the east, the coastal plain is fairly narrow, the escarpment rising abruptly, but sloping much more gently to the west, where there are expansive lowlands. An imposing mountain chain runs roughly down the centre of the island, but it has no really high peaks: the highest, **Mt Maromokotro**, is 2876m (9436ft).

The central highlands (Hauts Plateaux) vary in altitude from about 700–1500m (2300–5000ft) and are reached in some places after traversing a second escarpment or *tampoketsa*, meaning 'a plateau on a plateau'. The Hauts Plateaux feature grass-covered hills and valleys, with outcropping peaks consisting of rock such as granite, which is more resistant to erosion. Gaping amphitheatres or *lavaka* – a consequence of erosion – scar many hills in the countryside and are much in evidence, especially when flying over the countryside.

▶ Opposite: The Mandrare River snakes its way past Berenty Reserve and the Ifotaka Community Forest Site.
▼ Below: Fire-resistant Bismarkia palms dot the eerily silent landscape of the Horombe Plateau which borders the Isalo massif.

The west of Madagascar is of more recent origin and has some spectacular areas which have been strongly eroded into remarkable limestone formations chaotically decorated with friable, razor-sharp karstic pinnacles known as *tsingy* (a Malagasy reference to the noise produced when the pinnacles are struck). Between fortress-like limestone walls are sunken pockets of seasonally dry forest, while beneath them there are vast systems of caves, passages and subterranean rivers. The south is mostly semi-arid, and in the interior is a large sandstone massif with impressive *ruiniforme* formations.

Rivers

In Madagascar the east-flowing rivers are considerably shorter than those meandering west, the largest of these being the **Betsiboka**, which ends at the port of Mahajanga. The **Tsiribihina** ends north of Morondava at Belo sur Tsiribihina and the **Mangoky** snakes its way to the north of Morombe. The west-flowing **Manambolo** river passes through spectacular scenery, including imposing gorges and the Bemaraha Plateau.

On the narrow eastern coastal plain is the **Pangalanes Canal** (Lakandranon' Ampangalana), a waterway of some 600km (370 miles) connecting a system of lakes almost parallel to the east coast. It begins near the port of Toamasina (Tamatave) and continues all the way down to

Dangerous Areas in Madagascar

Madagascar is one of the world's poorest countries. It is understandable that tourists, or *vazaha*, may be viewed as 'walking banks'. Unfortunately, petty crime is on the increase, and in several places on the main tourist circuits it is now recommended that travellers are accompanied by a professional Malagasy guide and a driver. This applies in particular to the following areas: the RN7 route from Ranohira to Sakaraha, the sapphire town Ilakaka and St Augustin Bay; Analakely in Antananarivo; Montagne des Francais near Diégo Suarez, as well as the whole of Fort Dauphin.

the remote southeastern outpost of Vangaindrano. Partly man-made, it was used by boats in preference to the rough seas.

Seas and Shores

Madagascar lies in the western Indian Ocean (sometimes referred to historically as 'Sea of Zanj'), separated from Africa by the Mozambique Channel. Off the west coast, the continental shelf is broad and there are many islets and atolls. Coral reefs surround much of the island. The narrow east coastal shelf has a sandy sea bed with coral formations at some bays, coves and satellite islands.

Climate

Madagascar's climate is surprisingly **diverse**, emphasizing the concept of a mini-continent rather than just a single island. The bulk of the country lies within the **tropical zone**, with the Tropic of Capricorn cutting across the island just below Tuléar. Moisture-bearing trade winds from the Indian Ocean ensure year-round rainfall in the east (at least some rain may fall on an average of 320 days per annum), while the mountainous backbone prevents the same applying to the west where **rainfall** occurs mostly from December to April, peaking in January and February. In most years violent cyclones tear into parts of the island during the peak of the rains (late January to early March).

The wettest region is in the northeast, stretching from Maroantsetra northwards to the Marojejy massif. Here, the annual fall averages above 3000mm (118 in) and can reach 6000mm (236 in). In contrast, the Tuléar region of the southwest receives an average of 350mm (14 in) per annum, and nothing in some years. The interior escarpment and the high plateau regions have a seasonal, almost temperate climate, with frost often occurring in mid-winter and warm to hot days in

COMPARATIVE CLIMATE CHART	CENTRAL				NORTHERN				SOUTHERN			
	SUM	AUT	WIN	SPR	SUM	AUT	WIN	SPR	SUM	AUT	WIN	SPR
	JAN	APR	JULY	OCT	JAN	APR	JULY	OCT	JAN	APR	JULY	OCT
MAX TEMP. °C	17	21	32	23	12	20	34	23	15	24	36	26
MIN TEMP. °C	8	13	21	16	2	7	17	10	6	11	20	15
MAX TEMP. °F	63	70	70	73	54	68	93	73	59	75	97	79
MIN TEMP. °F	46	55	55	61	36	45	63	61	43	52	68	57
RAINFALL in	9.3	1	0.5	7.8	10	1.1	0.6	3.2	2.9	0.6	0.3	1.7
RAINFALL mm	235	26	12	197	274	28	16	81	73	16	7	44

Baobabs

Six of the world's eight baobab species are endemic to Madagascar. Malagasy refer to baobabs as *za* or *reniala*, meaning 'mother (or father) of the forest', and use parts of these succulent trees for building or weaving material, or food. The Alley of Giant Baobabs near Morondava is a much-photographed national monument and World Heritage Site. Here you can see:

- *Adansonia grandidieri* in the Menabe Protected Area, also Alley of Giant Baobabs.
- *A. za* near Berenty and around Zombitse-Vohibasia National Park.
- *A. rubrostipa*, the 'bottle tree', around Ifaty (common).
- *A. madagascariensis* at Anjajavy (abundant).
- *A. suarenzis* on dry hills around Diégo Suarez (highly range-restricted).
- *A. perrieri* in Montagne d'Ambre (extremely rare).

summer. Temperatures vary considerably across the different regions of Madagascar: in Antananarivo, at a height of 1380m (4525ft) above sea level, the average temperature varies from 16–19°C (60–66°F), and even in summer evenings can be cool. In the winter months on the eastern escarpment the temperature at night regularly goes as low as 3°C (37°F). In contrast, the western lowlands are hot, with temperatures of over 40°C (104°F) common in late spring and summer.

Plant Life

Madagascar is a botanist's dream, with its sharply contrasting climatic zones supporting equally diverse floral domains. The best known of Madagascar's habitat types is its **rainforest**, mostly concentrated in the damp eastern areas. These rainforests are among the world's densest and are distinguished by a lower canopy than those elsewhere in the tropics. In plant families such as palms and orchids, Madagascar's species totals far exceed those of the African continent. Madagascar accounts for only 2% of the African landmass, yet it possesses a staggering 20% of the vascular plant species, and of these, around 80% are found only on the island.

The largest example of lowland or coastal rainforest is on the **Masoala Peninsula** of the northeast. Some of the country's most visited hiking trails are in montane rainforest, which occurs between 800 and 1300m (2600 and 4300ft). Good examples are found in Andasibe-Mantadia (Périnet), Ranomafana and Montagne d'Ambre.

Perhaps the most fascinating of Madagascar's habitat types is the **spiny bush**, the bizarre vegetation of the semi-arid southern area. In its undis-

▼ Below: The very rare 'La Grande Orchidee Rose' may be seen at Andasibe-Mantadia National Park and on Ile Aux Nattes. It is one of the largest of Madagascar's 900-plus endemic orchid species.

The Aye Aye

The aye aye epitomizes Madagascar's weird and wonderful fauna. This gremlin-like nocturnal lemur has rodent-like incisors, bat-like ears, a huge, bushy tail and long, coarse fur. Its hands are unique, bearing no resemblance to any other animal. It uses its near-skeletal middle finger to extract invertebrates from trees. Because of its grotesque appearance, this elusive but widespread, cat-sized lemur is feared in parts of its natural range. It can be seen on the reserve island of Nosy Mangabe or on Aye Aye Island. Like some other nocturnal lemurs, the aye aye mostly forages alone, sleeping by day in nests concealed in tangled vegetation. It is the largest nocturnal primate.

turbed state it is a tangled arrangement of thorny, drought-resistant plants interspersed with bloated baobabs, pachypodiums, aloes and an abundance of euphorbias. Prominent in this habitat are the thorny didiera trees which include the octopus, finger and signature trees. At first glance some look like tall, slender cacti but they are true trees without the water-storing tissue of cacti. The best places for those interested in sub-desert flora are around Ifaty, Anakao, Tsimenampetsotsa and Ifotaka Community Forest.

Madagascar's third major forest type, the seasonally **dry** (deciduous) **forests**, exist in the western lowlands but they are extremely fragmented. A few of the remaining parcels receive protection: most accessible are Ankarafantsika, Kirindy (part of the large new Menabe Protected Area), the limestone plateaus of Bemaraha and Ankarana, and the privately protected tract Anjajavy. Towards the north, deciduous forests become less dry.

Wildlife

Despite its proximity to Africa, Madagascar has been split from the continent since the break-up of the super-continent Gondwana, and as a result all its non-flying, indigenous land mammals, 41% of its birds and more than 90% of its reptiles and 99% of its frogs are endemic. There are no indigenous hoofed animals (ungulates), and no true cats or dogs.

A good deal of attention is focused on the island's **lemurs**, a name which means 'souls of the dead reincarnated and living in the forest'. Lemurs range from the tailless, baboon-sized indri to the smallest of primates, Madame Berthe's mouse lemur, which averages 35g (1oz) in weight. In certain places lemurs have become habit-

▼ *Below: Western Madagascar's severely threatened and highly fragmented seasonally dry (deciduous) forests.*

◀ Left: Largest of the lemurs is the indri, which can only be seen in its natural home as it does not survive in captivity. Well habituated groups are easily seen at Andasibe-Mantadia National Park. Their siren-like calls are one of Madagascar's 'hallmark' sounds.

uated, much to the delight of visitors. To find such approachable lemurs you could go to Anjaha Community Conservation Site (ring-tailed lemurs); Lokobe (black lemurs); Berenty (ring-tailed lemurs, Verreaux's sifakas); Montagne d'Ambre (crowned lemurs); and Le Palmarium (black-and-white ruffed lemurs). Usually described as the largest lemur, the indri is easily seen in its rainforest home at Andasibe-Mantadia National Park (Périnet). Its calls are distinctive – a loud, siren-like howling, carrying for up to 3km (2 miles). Madagascar's national mammal is the iconic and highly terrestrial ring-tailed lemur.

There are over 40 species of tenrec, insectivores which in most cases resemble shrews and voles. Some look more like hedgehogs, being covered in spines and/or coarse fur. These include the common tenrec, the largest surviving Malagasy insectivore which also gives birth to the biggest litters of any mammal.

Of the other mammals, the endangered giant jumping rat (Madagascar's largest rodent) and the fosa – a predator resembling something between a mongoose, a weasel and a small, elongated puma – are among what visitors most want to see. Bats include the spectacular Madagascar fruit bat or 'flying fox', one of the westernmost representatives of an Asian genus with a wingspan of over a metre. About 35 of the ca. 46 known bat species are endemic. Most interesting are the rarely seen sucker-footed bats.

The Durrell Wildlife Conservation Trust

The DWCT was founded by the late Gerald Durrell, whose books did much to promote an international awareness of endangered Malagasy fauna. Their most publicized project is Projet Angonoka at Ankarafantsika National Park. Here, endangered endemic tortoises are breeding well, while work is conducted in their home ranges to educate and involve local communities in conservation programmes, ultimately securing a future for these species. The DWCT is also active in the vulnerable dry forests of Menabe. A selection of endangered or threatened Malagasy species such as aye aye, Alaotra gentle lemur, giant jumping rat and Madagascar teal are thriving at their Jersey Zoo. Lately they have also been participating in a project to breed the recently rediscovered Madagascar pochard. For more about the Trust's remarkable achievements, *see* www.durrell.org

▲ *Above: Largest of the 16-odd vangas is the sicklebilled vanga, a garrulous inhabitant of the dry western forests and southern bush. Its foraging habits are similar to those of Africa's wood-hoopoes.*
▶ *Opposite: A typical example of montane rainforest-clad hills and ridges in eastern Madagascar. Ranomafana and Andasibe-Mantadia national parks are among the most visited rainforest sites profiled in this book.*

Two hundred and ten of the 284 bird species recorded in Madagascar breed on the island, and of these 52% are endemic. The three unusual rail-like mesites are terrestrial and forest-dependent, flying only when hard pressed. Possibly even more peculiar than the mesites is the crow-sized cuckoo-roller, which eats chameleons, geckoes and large invertebrates. Other endemic families and subfamilies include the five attractive ground-rollers, the four asitys, the nine conspicuous couas, and the celebrated vangas, which range from the dove-sized sicklebilled vanga to the tiny nuthatch vanga. The vangas have radiated spectacularly to occupy niches left by shrikes, woodpeckers, woodhoopoes, tits and treecreepers.

The island has a rich herpetofauna (reptiles and frogs) and scientific surveys continue to reveal species new to science. More than 90% of the 400-plus reptile species are endemic. Madagascar holds more than half the world's chameleons (about 60 species), ranging from the gigantic Oustalet's and Parson's chameleons (both can reach a length of 68cm/26in) to the smallest, the 29mm (1.1 in) stump-tailed chameleon, *Brookesia micra*. The Malagasy geckoes enjoy a high profile because of the contrast between the conspicuous, green day-geckoes and the nocturnal leaf-tailed (*Uroplatus*) geckoes, which are among the most accomplished masters of camouflage in the animal kingdom. The 12 known *Uroplatus* species either mimic bark or dead leaves. Another interesting lizard group is the iguanids: they occur in Madagascar and South America, but not in Africa. Best known is the widespread collared iguanid with its black collar and spiny tail.

There are over 80 species of snake on Madagascar and many still await description. They include three boas, a family found in South America and Asia, but not Africa. The most commonly encountered colubrid snake is the giant hog-nosed snake, an attractive black-and-yellow species which is adept at ferreting out lizard eggs. In the absolutely remarkable spear-nosed snake, the male has a bayonette-shaped nasal extension and the female's looks like a fan. No Malagasy snake is dangerous, because front-fanged venomous snakes evolved after the island separated from the continents.

The world's rarest tortoise, the ploughshare or *angonoka*, is confined to the Soalala area in the remote western region. There are three other endangered and endemic tortoises and one endangered, endemic freshwater turtle, the *rere* (Madagascar big-headed turtle).

Madagascar lacks toads, newts and caecilians, but its frog species total is expected to reach 500 in the next few years. Found only in Torotorofotsy Marsh, the brightly coloured, endangered golden mantella is the island's flagship frog. Mantellas exhibit aposematic (warning) colouration as they are poisonous. This enables them to lead a diurnal existence. Numerous tree frogs can be seen and heard during night walks in the rainforests.

Habitat loss, wetland degradation and aggressive introduced exotic species have had a catastrophic effect on the island's endemic freshwater fish. They include various species of delicate rainbowfish, colourful killifish and some cichlids or *damba*. A few of these now survive only in captive-breeding progammes abroad.

Well-known species in the island's massive – and most likely very far from complete – catalogue of invertebrates include the lovely day-flying Urania moth, giraffe-necked weevil, the delightful hissing cockroach and the pill millipede. Less desirable invertebrates include mosquitoes, sand fleas and leeches.

Night Walks

At dusk a very different world comes to life in the forests of Madagascar. Because a large variety of Malagasy mammals, birds and 'herps' (reptiles and amphibians) are nocturnal, guided night strolls can be extremely interesting. In rainforests such as S.F. Analamazaotra (under Association Mitsinjo), and in other forests such as at Anjajavy or the gallery woods of Berenty, you may find a variety of nocturnal lemurs with ease. The fosa and giant jumping rat should be sought in Kirindy during November. Generally, night strolls reveal many 'herps' including wonderful nocturnal geckoes and tree frogs. Chameleons are also often seen as they initially reflect whitish in the beam of a torch. Take a strong flashlight with spare batteries.

The Bamboo Lemurs of Ranomafana

Ranomafana National Park is one of very few sites where three species of bamboo lemur coexist. The eastern lesser bamboo lemur is quite common, and increasingly visitors are seeing the endearing golden bamboo lemur, discovered here by Patricia Wright and Bernard Meier in 1986. It eats mainly the giant cyanide bamboo: its daily cyanide intake is enough to kill 30 humans. The greater bamboo lemur, however, is one of the rarest and among the most endangered of all primates. A Malagasy NGO, MICET (Madagascar Institute pour la Conservation des Environments Tropicaux), collaborating with the Institute for the Conservation of Tropical Environments (ICTE) – the university-based NGO of which Dr Wright is director – are working closely with Discover Life *(see* www.discoverlife.org) and Madagascar National Parks to acquire two small rainforest parcels outside Ranomafana, which they believe can secure the species' future. Dr Wright advises that Centre ValBio Conservation Hall will be open to tours in late 2011 and host public lectures by research scientists from 2012, to bridge the gap between research findings and international tourists.

Conserving Madagascar's Natural Heritage

'We can no longer afford to sit back and watch our forests go up in flame... We have the firm political will to stop this degradation' (President Marc Ravalomanana, 2003).

As anywhere on earth, man's arrival changed the face of the land he settled upon. First to go was the island's megafauna, but investigations suggest that those species were already heading for natural extinction due to significant climate changes. With man came non-sustainable agricultural practices from Asia (*tavy* or slash-and-burn) and the near-sacred Zebu cattle, which symbolize wealth and are a link with the ancestors.

From 1960–85, half the forests were cleared as the population doubled and the economy spiralled downwards. In the 1970s, Madagascar was recognized by international conservation agencies as one of the world's six areas of 'megadiversity' but also as one whose natural assets are most at risk. It is one of the world's most eroded countries and much of the countryside is covered in short, tough grasses or *bozaka*.

Already in the 1920s, the French set aside 10 protected areas. In 1988, the World Bank published a 20-year Environmental Action Plan and the WWF initiated a Debt for Nature swap (where part of Madagascar's debt would be written off against protected areas being established) in 1989. The long-term goal is upliftment of poverty and

▶ *Right: A natural history guide is planting an endangered sapling from the tree nursery at Vohibola, managed by the NGO MATE.*

fostering of self-sufficiency among the Malagasy people. Particular emphasis is laid on the implementation of sustainable agricultural techiques. Madagascar National Park, formerly known as The National Association for Management of Protected Areas (ANGAP) is responsible for administering most of the protected areas and half of the fees from park permits are ploughed back into communities living around protected sites. Many NGOs from around the world are involved in the conservation of Madagascar's natural assets.

▲ *Above: Tombstone with skull and crossbones in the pirates' cemetery on Ste Marie Island, formerly the most prominent of the many pirate hide-outs around Madagascar.*

In 2003, President Ravalomanana undertook to increase the protected areas from 1.6 million hectares to over 6 million hectares by 2008, meaning an increase from 3% to 10% of the country's surface area. The various categories of protected area were then grouped into the System of Protected Areas of Madagascar. Other aims of the conservation programme include protection of the cultural heritage, development of ecotourism (and becoming a regional leader in that arena), increased protection of watersheds, and the establishment of forest corridors to link isolated forest blocks. Most progress on the conservation front however, ground to a halt after the change of government in March 2009, and the level of commitment on the part of the current interim government to conservation – and indeed to the well-being of the Malagasy nation as a whole – remains to be seen. At time of writing (January 2013) this is still the case.

HISTORY IN BRIEF

Early Settlement

Madagascar was one of the last habitable landmasses to have been settled by man, with most authorities agreeing that the first settlers arrived on outrigger canoes from Polynesia, Melanesia and Indonesia about 2000 years ago. The original inhabitants, the **Vazimba**, were likely

Tomb Architecture

The *razana* (ancestors) are eternal so it follows that they should be comfortably housed. For this reason tombs are generally more solid and expensive than homes of the living. Merina tombs are four-cornered, with the bulk built underground. Decorated inside, their size indicates family wealth. Originally simple stone piles, Sakalava tomb design changed with the introduction of cement. Wooden stelae (*aloalo*) of 1.5m (5ft) are placed on tombs in the south. Stelae are topped by carvings which in Menabe Sakalava are of an erotic nature. Zebu horns on Mahafaly and Antandroy tombs indicate wealth and status of the person interred.

absorbed into the contemporary tribes (the Malagasy use the term 'tribes' freely). Where Indonesian influence is noticeable is in the use of agricultural techniques like rice cultivation, modes of transport such as the *balancier*

HISTORICAL CALENDAR

500–600 First (presumed) settlement of Madagascar.
1500 Diego Dias 'discovers' Madagascar by accident.
1650s Formation of the Sakalava Kingdoms (Menabe followed by Boina).
1716 Confederation of Betsimisaraka people on east coast.
1777 Mayeur, a French slave trader and the first European to penetrate the interior highland, delivers a report on the isolated Imerina people to the world.
1780 Andrianampoinimerina first king of the Merina people.
1795 Antananarivo designated as the Malagasy capital.
1810 Radama I elected Merina king and rules until 1828.
1828–61 Rule of the 'Pagan Queen' Ranavalona I. By the 1830s the Merina dominate over most of Madagascar.
1835 Christianity outlawed.
1836 Most Europeans leave Madagascar.
1861 Radama II becomes Merina king. Freedom of religion proclaimed, missionaries are re-admitted into Madagascar.
1863 Radama II is assassinated, succeeded by Queen Rasoherina.
1883 Ranavalona III becomes queen. The Franco-Hova War starts and ends in 1885.
1895 Madagascar becomes a French protectorate. In 1896 it becomes a full colony.
1896 First stage of the Malagasy Nationalist Movement, the Menalamba, started.
1897 Abolition of the Merina monarchy by the French. Queen Ranavalona III is exiled.
1942 British occupation.
1947 Malagasy nationalist rebellion suppressed.
1960 Madagascar achieves full independence (26 June). Philibert Tsiranana becomes president of the First Republic.
1962 Government takes over internal air network and Ivato International Airport is built.
1972 General Ramanantsoa assumes power and paves the way for the birth of the Second Republic. Tsiranana forced to step down as president in May.
1975 Didier Ratsiraka is elected president. Madagascar embraces his brand of 'Christian-Marxism'. Deterioration in relations with Europe. Bonds strengthened with USSR, China, North Korea.
1976 All larger commercial concerns nationalized.
1984 Loan negotiated with the World Bank and standby support from the IMF. Defence is a major recipient of government money.
1991 Prolonged strikes and demonstrations organized by pro-democracy 'Forces Vivres' bring economy to a standstill. The movement, under Guy Razamanasy, facilitates the transition to the Third Republic. Ratsiraka is forced to step down.
1993 Albert Zafy is president.
1993 Birth of the Third Republic (democratic).
1996 Zafy steps down. Didier Ratsiraka is re-elected in 1997.
2001 Marc Ravalomanana wins presidential election. Ratsiraka refuses to accept.
2002 The 'political crisis' lasts from Jan–July. Ravalomanana's position of president accepted by USA, Switzerland and the UK. Eventually France and the African Union (AU) follow.
2003 Ravalomanana commences the restoration and upgrading of Madagascar's infrastructure and announces his commitment to upliftment of poverty and preservation of the country's natural heritage.
2006 Ravalomanana is re-elected for his second term and shifts focus to the Madagascar Action Plan (MAP).
2009 Former mayor of Antananarivo, Andry Rajoelina ousts democratically elected Ravalomanana and declares himself leader of the High Transitional Authority without recognition from the international community
2011 Eight political parties sign agreement to pave way for elections to be held 'within a year' to re-establish democracy. A new unity government is unveiled. Opposition parties agree to join 'without hesitation'. Former president Ratsiraka returns after nine years in exile.
2012 Rajoelina announces he hopes elections will take place 'as soon as possible'.

pirogue and four-cornered dwellings (an Asian architectural style which predominates over round huts of Africa).

Later influences came from Africa and from Arab traders sailing south from East Africa in search of convenient bases for the slave trade. Europe discovered Madagascar on 10 August 1500, when the Portuguese sailor Diego Dias inadvertently ended up on Madagascar's coast. It was only when he was on his way back home that he realized that the place where he had landed was not Africa, and he named the landmass St Laurent.

The island proved a useful strategic base for pirates, who were able to prey on ships crossing the Indian Ocean to and from the spice islands of the East Indies, and over the next two centuries a mixture of Portuguese, Italian and British riffraff frequented the east coast, with Ste Marie Island being one of their more celebrated strongholds. To these early settlers, traders and explorers the island was considered hostile, especially after a group of Portuguese settlers was massacred by the Antanosy (a southern Malagasy tribe) in 1528. It wasn't till the late 18th century, when a slave trader, Mayeur, explored the inland that the West came to learn of the Merina and Betsileo living in the interior uplands.

Useful Malagasy Phrases

Mbola tsara • hello (east coast)
Manao ahoana • hello
Veloma • goodbye
Azafady • please/excuse me
Tsara be • very good
Tsy misy • (I have) nothing
Ny anarako • My name is
Iza no anaranao? • What's your name?
Misaotra • thanks
Vizaka aho • I'm tired
Manetaheta aho • I'm thirsty
Noana aho • I'm hungry
Misy toerana hatoriana ve? • Is there place to sleep?

Rise of the Merina

Although a number of clans dominated various areas of Madagascar at different times, two tribes, the **Sakalava** and the **Merina**, played the most prominent role in shaping Malagasy history. The Sakalava originated in the west of Madagascar, and much of their influence came through combining small splinter groups and tribes and extending a network of trade. The Merina, on the other hand, who originated in the highlands around the present capital, Antananarivo, expanded by dominating neighbouring tribes.

In the 1790s, a chief of one of the smaller Merina clans, Andrianampoinimerina ('the hope of Imerina'), largely united his people. He moved his base to Antananarivo,

▼ Below: A colourful Sakalava mural.

Place Names

Many towns or regions have Malagasy and French names, both of which are used today. This is a list of such places on the popular tourist routes.

Malagasy • French
Antananarivo (Tana) • Tananarive
Analamazaotra/Andasibe • Périnet
Nosy Boraha • Ste Marie
Mahajanga • Majunga
Toliara • Tuléar
Tôlañaro • Fort Dauphin
Antsirañana • Diégo Suarez
Anantsono • St Augustin
Andoany • Hell-Ville
Mahavelona • Foulpoint
Iharana • Vohemar (part of the northeastern 'SAVA' region)
Ambohitra • Joffreville

ousting the town's inhabitants and indicated his intention to dominate the entire island by proclaiming that the Merina kingdom would have no boundary but the sea. His young son and successor, Radama I, ruled from 1810–28 and started forging relations with the Europeans, whom his father had scorned. At the time there was a protracted rivalry between the French and British for Madagascar, which was viewed as an untapped source of produce and slave labour. Both planned to control the western Indian Ocean from their respective bases in Réunion and Mauritius.

Radama I continued the expansion of the Merina kingdom, conquering the Betsileo, Betsimisaraka and Boina Sakalava people. He signed a Treaty of Alliance in 1817 with Britain, advocating a mutual friendship, the abolition of slavery and compensation to Radama for the costs involved in stamping out slavery and the threat of Sakalava pirates.

In 1818, the first missionaries from the London Missionary Society were welcomed by Radama on their arrival in Madagascar. The first printing press was introduced in 1826, and by the end of Radama's rule, literacy and Christianity had spread among the Malagasy.

▶ *Opposite: The prime minister's palace on a hill overlooking Tana.*
▼ *Below: The Rova or royal palace before the 1995 fire. It is slowly being restored.*

Queen Ranavalona

Radama I did not leave a male heir – or so it was claimed – and the formidable Hova aristocracy selected Ranavalona, one of Radama's widows, as his successor. The Hova aristocracy, keen to grab more power, murdered many of Radama's supporters and relatives, including the very young legal heir, Rakotobe.

One of Ranavalona's first moves was to sever ties between Madagascar and Britain. In 1829 she notified Lyall, the then British representative, of her repudiation of the 1817 Treaty

of Alliance, and he left Madagascar soon afterwards. The French government was reluctant to get involved, preferring to avoid trouble with Britain. But the French on Réunion, desperate to use the opportunity to tap the resources of Madagascar, sent a garrison to Foulpoint. The garrison was trapped in an ambush, the casualties were beheaded, and their heads placed on spears on the beach.

Ranavalona's 33-year rule, from 1828–61, was marked by the persecution of Christians and a deterioration of relations with all foreigners. Resilient Christians kept their faith secret and if exposed, they were speared to death or bound and rolled off the high cliffs on which the royal palace, the Rova, is built.

Among the few Europeans who remained in Madagascar was Jean Laborde. He had arrived in 1831, employed by Ranavalona to make guns. Using forced labour, the queen sent 2000 workers to Laborde, who manufactured weaponry, glass, lime, paint, ink, bricks, tiles, sugar and potash. He also introduced sheep, apples and grapes to Madagascar and built palaces for Ranavalona. Meanwhile, the French gained a stronghold when they established a base on the island of Nosy Bé. The increasingly intolerant attitude of the Hova towards Europeans aggravated the French and British, who combined forces to attack the port of Toamasina. Three warships flattened the port and 350 troops attacked the Arab-built fort, but they were eventually repelled and the heads of the 21 dead troops were displayed on spears at the beach. The Hova banned trade with the outside world for eight years.

In 1857, a plot to overthrow Ranavalona, involving Lambert (one of only six Europeans in Tana at the time) and the young heir, Radama II, was uncovered by the

Malagasy Cultural Events

The Antakarana people of the northwest are probably best known for their *tsanga-tsaine* rituals, during which two slender trees are tied together, bridging the gap between the past and present, and between the living and ancestors. In June, the Betsimisaraka engage in tomb-cleansing (*tody tranomara*). Also during June or July, the Menabe Sakalava hold *fitampoha* every 10 years, during which the royal relics are taken to a river and washed. Among Boina Sakalava it is called *fanampoahambe*. The highlands people conduct their *famadihana* ceremonies (second burial) from June through September. The remains of a selected departed relative are removed from the family tomb, rewrapped in a new burial shroud, and reinterred in the tomb.

▲ *Above: Madagascar's earliest church was built in 1857 on Ste Marie after the arrival of Welsh missionaries of the London Missionary Society.*
▶ *Opposite: Stone commemorating the 1947 rebellion during which many Malagasy were killed.*

queen, and all foreigners were banished. Those bound for exile were forced to walk from Tana to Toamasina under constant guard. Most contracted malaria during the gruelling 53-day journey. An intrepid globetrotter, Ida Pheiffer, was among this group. She left behind a vivid account of the above-mentioned plot and of the journey to the east coast. In her extraordinary memoirs, she wrote: 'With a truly heartfelt joy, I turned my back on a place where I had suffered so much'.

Ranavalona was succeeded by her son, Radama II, who proclaimed freedom of religion during his short rule. He opted for reform, released political prisoners and re-opened trade with the Mascarenes. Immediately, exiles such as Laborde and Lambert returned, but this brought about jealousy among the aristocracy. In 1863, the aristocracy raided the palace and strangled Radama II in front of his wife, Rabodo, who was terrified into submission. She became Queen Rasoaherina but was little more than a figurehead. She married the brilliant Hova prime minister, Rainilaiarivory, who also married the next two Merina queens, Ranavalona II and III.

During the reign of Rasoaherina, Christianity became the gateway to Westernization and missionaries flooded into Madagascar. When Rasoaherina died in 1868 the Hova elected her cousin, the 39-year-old Ramona, as Queen Ranavalona II (1868–83). A Christian educated by the London Missionary Society and known for her exceptional compassion, she ordered that all *sampy* (objects or idols associated with the traditional religion) be burned, and in 1869 Protestantism was declared the single form of religion. Relations with France improved, and by 1877 the Arab slave trade on Madagascar had been stamped out and all African slaves released and given the status of free citizens.

By 1883, however, when Ranavalona II was succeeded by her 22-year-old niece, Razafindranety, who became Ranavalona III, the relationship between the Hova and the French had deteriorated again, prompting the French to attack the port of Mahajanga. In the face of French aggression the British were covertly supporting the Hova with arms and troops who arrived from South Africa under the command of a Colonel Digby Willoughby. He impressed the Hova and became their army commander. In 1894, the French sent an ultimatum to the Hova aristocrats demanding full control over Madagascar. Under the experienced General Duchesne, they made a full-scale attack, using the Betsiboka River as their entry route. The Hova aristocrats fled and the Merina army was left leaderless. The Merina had only the London Missionary Society and their biggest ally, *tazo* (fever or malaria), as support. Malaria claimed the lives of more than 6000 French troops, but the invaders soon took control, removing both the prime minister and, in a move designed to break the spirit of the Merina, they abolished the monarchy. In October 1895, Madagascar became a French protectorate.

Didier Ratsiraka

The former president and now in exile, Ratsiraka ruled over Madagascar with a vice-like grip for 23 years. During his time as president the economy collapsed and corruption ran riot. Ratsiraka was accused of stealing US$ 8,000,000 of public money from the central bank in 2002, shortly before he went into exile. In his absence, he has been sentenced to 10 years of hard labour. The court also issued a national arrest warrant for Mr Ratsiraka and declared him unfit for public office. Ratsiraka's former finance minister, Blandin Razafinjato, and the central bank governor, Ferdinand Velomita, were jailed in their absence for six years.

Malagasy Independence

Though frequently suppressed by the French, Malagasy nationalism grew under colonial rule, until in the 1940s and '50s when there was marked discontent among the Malagasy towards the French. Demands for independence grew after World War II. A referendum was held in 1958 and on 26 June 1960, the country gained independence.

The First Republic, the République Malgache, had Philibert Tsiranana as its president (1960–72), although the French still ruled in practice. On 13 May 1972, a revolution broke out and Tsiranana was forced to resign. A military *directoire* led by General Gilles Andriamahazo marked the start of a transition period (1972–75); he was succeeded by General Ramanantsoa, who prepared the way for the Second Republic.

The Second Republic of Madagascar had two presidents: the first was Richard Ratsimandrava, who was assassinated after five

TOTAL NUMBER OF TOURISTS TO MADAGASCAR IN 2012

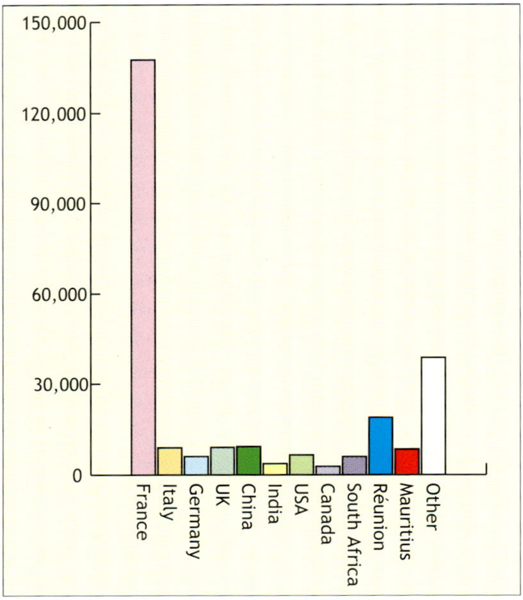

days in office, and on 15 June 1975, Admiral Didier Ratsiraka assumed authority over the country, now known as the République Democratique de Madagascar. The country embraced socialism, or rather Ratsiraka's own brand of it, Christian-Marxism. There were numerous severe socio-economic crises during the rule of Ratsiraka, along with a deterioration in relations with Europe as strong ties were forged with the Soviet-bloc nations, Korea and Libya. In 1991, after 16 years of dictatorship, there was a series of strikes which brought the Malagasy economy to a virtual standstill. These strikes were led by the HAE (Haute Autorité d'Etat) under Guy Razamanasy, a member of the Hova aristocracy who prepared the way for the Third Republic by organizing an election. On 10 February 1993 Professor Albert Zafy, a surgeon, became president of the Third Republic, République de Madagascar.

In September 1996, Prof Zafy was removed from office. The elections which followed had Didier Ratsiraka reinstated as president for another five years. Activities in the December 2001 elections would eventually bring the country to a spectacular halt. Accusations of vote rigging during the first round led to a second round being called. Supporters of the two leading candidates – Ratsiraka and the Mayor of Antananarivo, wealthy businessman Marc Ravalomanana – clashed to the point of civil unrest. Attempts by the African Union (AU) and the UN to encourage peace failed.

In April 2002, after Ratsiraka and Ravalomanana met in Dakar, a recount of votes from the first round of elections was arranged. Ravalomanana was revealed as the winner and he was inaugurated as president on 7 May 2002. Ratsiraka, however, refused to step down and moved to Toamasina, his coastal stronghold. (So, for a brief period, Madagascar had two capitals and two presidents.) Ratsirakists isolated Antananarivo by setting up military roadblocks and destroying bridges, depriving residents of essential goods, severing trade and creating serious and lasting problems for the economy. Many a business went bankrupt that year. But Ravalomanana's support base expanded steadily. Daily his supporters demonstrated and marched peacefully in the streets of Antananarivo. The USA, Switzerland and the UK were among the first to acknowledge the new president. France, which had strong links with Ratsiraka, dithered for some time before formally following suit, as did countries in the AU, whose leaders were part of a circle of dictators.

Marc Ravalomanana – the first Merina ever to be elected president – was re-elected for a second, five-year term after a win of 54.8% in December 2006. During his second term, however, an ever-increasing undercurrent of discontent rumbled on in Madagascar and in March 2009, Ravalomanana was ousted in a coup by former mayor of Antananarivo, Andry Rajoelina, who had secured the backing of the military through his powerful French and other, political connections. The Presidential palace was stormed, the central bank raided and on 21 March 2009 the 36-year-old former disc jockey declared himself president. Western countries froze all but some humanitarian aid, and Madagascar was suspended from the AU and SADC.

In 2011, eight political parties signed an agreement in support of elections to re-establish democracy. However, these have been postponed on a number of occasions, Rajoelina stating in 2012 that elections will take place 'as soon as possible'. 2011 also saw the return of Ratsiraka after nine years in exile. In 2012, however, Ravalomanana's attempt to return was thwarted.

Invest in a Zebu!

Zebu symbolize wealth and a link with the ancestors. They are present at most religious ceremonies. Their lyre-shaped horns decorate many tombs. When sacrificed, zebu heads are given to the highest-ranking community members. At some ceremonies zebu blood is smeared on the bodies of attendants for purification and zebu fat is used to make incense. Through the Zebu Overseas Board (ZOB), friends of Madagascar may now invest in a zebu. Your zebu is leased to an impoverished rural family, who use it to produce milk, plough fields, breed cattle, pull carts and produce fertiliser. You then earn a Solidarity Overseas Bond or 'SOB'. After a monthly reimbursement period over two to three years, the farmer takes ownership. ZOB aims to assist disadvantaged farmers, who do not have any other financial institution to assist them. While promoting organic farming and traditional rearing, ZOB is an original financing concept, where the investor has a link with the user of the funds. The investor has the host family's address, and is kept informed about the uses of the zebu. The ZOB encourages the investor to visit their zebu, rub its nose and enquire about its health. Sympathetic towards the suffering investors endure by being so far from their investment, ZOB post photos of the zebu on their website: www.zob-madagascar.org

▶ *Right: Madagascar is the world's largest vanilla-producing country. The industry is concentrated in the humid northeast.*

GOVERNMENT AND ECONOMY

The Republic of Madagascar is governed by a presidential system, and is currently divided into six administrative provinces (*faritany mizakatena*): Antananarivo, Antsirañana, Fianarantsoa, Mahajanga, Toamasina and Toliara. These provinces are divided into 22 regions, which are again subdivided into 116 districts, 1548 communes and 16,969 *fokontany*. The chief of state is the president and head of government the prime minister, appointed by the president. The prime minister appoints a council of ministers who form the cabinet. Presidential elections are held every five years, but since Andry Rajoelina assumed his current position of leader of the High Transitional Authority, dates of future elections are never a certainty.

During President Ravalomanana's first term in office, free market reforms were applauded by investors; debts were cancelled and aid to the country was increased. But the new democratic government inherited a ruined economy, and there has been continued discontent over ever-increasing prices of basic goods and services.

For his second term, President Ravalomanana is focusing on the bold and ambitious MAP (Madagascar Action Plan), a five-year plan dedicated to reducing poverty by 50%. The first of the MAP's eight commitments, responsible governance, is expressed as follows: 'We will have a government

Collateral Damage

From February to November 2009, an estimated 4000 containers of precious timber, each valued at US$200,000 were exported, mostly from Vohemar. That is, a total of US$800,000,000! Four thousand containers can accommodate 520,000 logs or 'bola-bola', which accounts for some 260,000 trees. But the collateral damage ought to be taken into account too: to float each heavy log, five lightweight trees and forest lianas are used to make rafts.

that every citizen and the international community can trust and have confidence in. This government and civil service will have integrity, be efficient and act totally professionally in all pursuits, activities and the provision of service.'

One of seven challenges to be dealt with under responsible governance is a massive crackdown on corruption, which was rife during Ratsiraka's dictatorial rule. Another of the commitments is the decentralization of government administration. Widespread reform is planned for the judicial system, trials are to be fast-tracked, transparent and fair. Legislation is being shaped to address needs of rapid development. Respect will be upheld for the UN Human Rights Charter. There is also a commitment to create an education system of international standard. It is planned to transform the economy into one of high growth, with growth rates 'reaching between 7 and 10% by 2012'. Here challenges include increasing foreign investment, ensuring a macro-economic environment conducive to business development, a reformation of the financial and banking system, and intensive development of both the tourism and mining sectors.

Potentially wealthy, Madagascar is currently one of the world's poorest countries following economic decline during the Ratsiraka era, and notably following the 2009 change of government which saw growth in economic output decline to under 1%. Since the Ratsiraka era, economic gains have inevitably been consumed by corruption, low foreign reserves and a fast-growing population, now estimated at 23 million. About 90% of the population survive on less than US$2 a day.

From the mid-1990s Madagascar has been following a World Bank and IMF-led policy of liberalization and privatization. This welcome change from former socialist economic policies has finally placed the country on a slow, but steady path of economic growth. Impressive improvements in this regard, particularly during the first term of former president Ravalomanana, were followed by a rapid decline as foreign investment dwindled sharply after the events of March 2009; tourism decreased drastically in 2009 to less than 35% of what it had been in 2008 (but picked up again in 2010 and increased steadily in 2011 and 2012). The

The Rosewood Massacre and Rosewood President

The 2009 political fallout spelled disaster for Madagascar's fragile forests, notably those in the UNESCO World Heritage Site of Antsirañana, a cluster of rainforests including the national parks of Masoala and Marojejy. Species targeted are the endemic rosewoods and ebonies.

'Madagascar's tourism industry annually brings nearly a half-billion US dollars to tens of thousands of people involved in all aspects of the industry,' reported Hery Randriamalala and Zhou Liu in 'Madagascar Conservation & Development Journal' (www.mwc-info.net/en/services/journal.htm), which in June 2010 published the most detailed report of the illegal logging fiasco. By contrast, the illegal high-end timber industry has resulted in a one-time windfall of an estimated $ US 220 million for just 23 individuals.

On 16 November 2010 Rhett Butler's leading rainforest conservation site (www.mongabay.com) reported ongoing, extensive logging, wildlife poaching and forest degradation in Madagascar's national parks despite a moratorium signed by the Malagasy government in March 2010 prohibiting further felling, transporting and export of rosewoods and ebonies. This followed the discovery of 10,000 people illegally logging in Masoala National Park.

▲ *Above: A wide range of minerals can be purchased at the Artisans' Market in Tana.*

cutting of almost all bilateral aid has had serious effects on this donor-dependent nation, of which the IMF estimates donor assistance accounted for some 80% of the island's budget and of government investment.

What then, were the main reasons for the decline in support of the 61-year-old, self-made multi-millionaire Marc Ravalomanana? Many hold the opinion that, as a businessman, he sought to run the country in an increasingly autocratic manner, and two enormous mistakes he made were, firstly, an attempt to sign off a staggering 3.2 million acres (almost half of the country's arable land) to the South Korean conglomerate Daewoo on a 99-year lease, primarily for the cultivation of corn and palm oil and secondly, the purchase of a presidential jet for US$60 million. To date he has been sentenced three times in absentia: first for life in prison and hard labour for the deaths of 30 protesters killed by presidential guards when they stormed the palace in February 2009; secondly he received a four-year jail sentence and a fine connected with the purchase of the jet, and he has also been sentenced to five years' hard labour over the land-grab deal attempt with South Korea.

Working Holidays

For those who wish to put something back while gaining a wonderful learning experience, organizations such as Earthwatch have offered marvellous scientific research trips with renowned lemur experts such as Lady Alison Jolly (Berenty), author of *Lords and Lemurs*, and Dr Patricia Wright (Ranomafana) – see www.earthwatch.org/europe For adventurous and active travellers interested in contributing to marine conservation, the award-winning, not-for-profit organization Blue Ventures is based at beautiful and remote Andavadoaka on the southwest coast: they work with teams of volunteers, local communities and NGOs. For their expedition dates, *see* www.blueventures.org

Agriculture

About 85% of Madagascar's population lives in rural areas – agriculture has always been a mainstay of the economy. Rice, the staple diet, accounts for about half of the country's agricultural output, with cassava, sugar, maize and coffee being other significant crops. Cloves, cotton, tobacco and tropical fruit (notably lychees) are grown for export. Madagascar is the world's largest producer of **vanilla**, accounting for half of the international export market. (It is mainly used for Coca-Cola.) Formerly a rice exporter, Madagascar must now import rice because of growers having reverted largely to subsistence farming. Prawns are farmed along the west coast. Currently the main exports include vanilla, seafood, cloves (production of which declined massively in 2010), petroleum products, chromium, fabrics and coffee.

Mineral Deposits

There are deposits of nickel, mica, bauxite, coal and tar sand, as well as chromite, graphite, gold and garnets on the island. Formerly, mineral exploitation was restricted by technical difficulties in mining, uncertain market opportunities, poor transport and poor power supplies. But mining operations are now under way near Fort Dauphin (following years of planning and preparation by Rio Tinto/QMM) to exploit ilmenite deposits, and at Ambatovy (80km east of Antananarivo) where the Sherrit mining project (nickel and cobalt) – which has a projected cost of US$ 6.3 billion – represents the largest foreign investment yet in Madagascar. Other mining operations are involved with the exploitation of graphite and bauxite. These activities could make a major difference to the economy. There are plans to mine coal, and Madagascar Oil is developing two oil fields. Indiscriminate and uncontrolled small-scale mining has, however, in recent times wreaked havoc in areas such as Daraina and Andasibe-Mantadia.

Industry

A relatively small but expanding industrial base – the industrial growth rate in 2010 was 2% (down from 6% in 2007) – means Madagascar still has to import petroleum, western medication and chemicals. Existing industry includes processing of agricultural products and textile manufacturing.

Industrial centres are mostly around Antananarivo, Antsirabe and the main port, Toamasina. A lack of reliable domestic transportation has hitherto hampered the progress of industrialization. In 2000, industry accounted for about 11% of GDP. Many plants have been operating at less than 30% of their capacity. Ammonia-based fertilizers have been produced since the mid-1980s and Madagascar produces pulp for paper and cement. There are cotton weaving and spinning plants and automobile assembling plants. In 2012, leading import partners were China (17.4%), France (13.2%), South Africa (6.7%), and Singapore (4.9%).

FIHAVANANA: BASED ON RESPECT

Malagasy social life is centred around *fihavanana*, a philosophy based on respect of family links and tradition, altruism, tolerance and blessing from the ancestors (*razana*). Various rites or events mark the Malagasy path, from birth to physical death and beyond. These include *famorana* (circumcision), *vodiondry* (the engagement ceremonial), and *famadihana* (exhumation or second burial). Oral tradition involves a catalogue of stories and legends through which ancestral wisdom and social bonds are perpetuated. Traditional values are reflected in *kabary*, a form of speech making use of proverbs (*ohabolana*) and metaphors (*hainteny*). While there are regional differences, the Malagasy are united by language and culture.

▲ *Above: A class at Centre Fihavanana (Antananarivo), a project assisted by the charity* Money For Madagascar, *whose policy is to support projects initiated and run by the Malagasy themselves.*

Infrastructure

In 1999, Madagascar had 49,827km (30,962 miles) of roads, of which 5780km (3592 miles) were paved. This figure is now much higher, as infrastructural upgrading was implemented surprisingly quickly by the proactive Ravalomanana government. Repair work is often held back by weather, especially cyclones. Climate, which can affect many routes by making them impassable, has had a significant bearing on internal communications. This is partly compensated for by an extensive domestic air network, with 104 airports, of which 77 do not have paved runways. There are 854km (530 miles) of railways.

The main port, Tamatave (Toamasina), on the east coast, handles most of the maritime traffic. It has links to Antananarivo by rail and road. The more indented west coast has several harbours, largest of which are Mahajanga and Tuléar.

Vakana

The strings of colourful beads in the picture on page 34 are called *vakana*. These beads come in a huge variety of colours, shapes and sizes. Each bead has its own meaning, or represents a particular aspect of life. To find out which *vakana* they should wear, people consult with their *Ombiasy* (wise person), who will suggest an appropriate combination of the beads depending on the person's circumstances. The 'language' of *vakana* is interesting and complex: many beads have male and female variants, which should be worn together. And all are 'activated' by the disk-shaped beads called *felana*.

Education and Training

Recent estimates give an adult literacy rate of 68.9% (figure for the total population).

Education is compulsory for children between the ages of six and 14. The current system provides primary schooling for five years, from ages six to 11. Secondary education lasts for seven years, divided into two parts: a junior secondary level of four years from ages 12 to 15, and a senior secondary level of three years from ages 16 to 18. At the end of the junior level, graduates receive a certificate, and at the end of the senior level, they receive a baccalaureate. The University of Madagascar has six campuses: Antananarivo, Antsirañana/Diégo Suarez, Fianarantsoa, Toamasina, Toliara, and Mahajanga. Faculties include law, economics and science. There are schools specializing in public administration, management, medicine and social welfare, and there are teacher training colleges. Reform measures are under way to improve the success rate of students, because only a small percentage have been completing their programmes. Many students complete degrees abroad, mainly in France. Malagasy is the first language and French the business language.

THE PEOPLE

Tribal Groupings

It is generally believed that the **Malagasy** people are descendants of the Malay-Polynesians who migrated from Southeast Asia roughly 2000 years ago. More immigrants arrived from Arabia and Africa and subsequently made their mark, especially on local customs that are still carried out today.

The Malagasy, although united by language and culture, show many regional differences among the various tribes. Most sources suggest that there are 18 major tribes, as well as numerous smaller sub-tribes and clans.

The people of the highlands (**Merina** and the related **Betsileo**) portray more Malayo-Indonesian characteristics, while among the coastal tribes (**Sakalava** and **Betsimisaraka**, particularly) and southern tribes (especially **Bara** and **Antandroy**) they display distinctly African characteristics. In addition, there are substantial Indian, Creole, Comoran, Chinese and French communities. The contemporary groups inhabit the following

Famadihana: Turning of the Bones

Among the Merina people, *famadihana* are often held following the transmission of a message by a *razana* (ancestral spirit) to one of their descendants. The *razana* will sometimes ask to be re-wrapped in such communication. Most *famadihana* last three days. Before the event, the selected ancestral spirit must be informed as to the date, so that it does not wander from the family tomb before or during the event. The attendants will then gather around the tomb, and the selected ancestor's remains will be removed and placed on a *tsihy* (grass mat). The procession then takes the remains around the tomb seven times, to remind the ancestral spirit that this is their home. The remains are then wrapped from left to right, in an even number. The remains will be danced with, spoken with, and asked for blessings before being reinterred head-first into the tomb.

Left: During this bone-turning ceremony the young women take small pieces of the shroud which they later put under their mattresses in order to induce fertility.

▲ *Above: A Mahafaly tomb in the southern semi-desert with typically colourful artwork and zebu horns.*

regions: the **Sakalava** in the west and northwest; the **Antakarana** and **Tsimehety** in the north; the **Merina**, **Betsileo**, **Sihanaka** and **Bezanozano** in the highlands and eastern interior; the **Betsimisaraka** in the central east and northeast; the **Antandroy**, **Bara**, **Mahafaly** and **Masikoro** in the southwest; and the **Antanosy**, **Antaisaka**, **Antaifasy**, **Antamboahaka** and **Tanala** in the southeast. Most tribes are subdivided into sub-tribes (e.g. **Boina** and **Menabe Sakalava**) and numerous clans, which may form at any time and take their names from any attribute they choose to.

A Traditional Culture

The traditional religion of the Malagasy is based on reverence of the ancestors, or *razana*. It is perhaps best known through the practice of bone-turning ceremonies, or *famadihana*, when the remains of a selected relative are exhumed, passed among the guests and filled in on the latest developments. These are intense occasions, including much celebration.

The Malagasy call the soul *ambiroa*. It can separate from the body in the dream state and leaves forever at death. At this point it becomes a *razana*, which is immortal. It is believed that if a person dies far from their home town, the body must be brought back to that town for burial or else the soul will wander until the remains are returned home.

Deities

Almost all Malagasy combine the Christian faith (either Catholic or Protestant) with their traditional religion. Two old groups, the Antalaotra in the northwest and the Antaimoro ('Arab-Malagasy') of the southeast, adopted Muslim practices. In the traditional religion, the Highest Being or Creator is Zanihari, or Andriananahary, now referred to as Andriamanitra, who is neither male nor female. There are a

Malagasy Pronunciations

Pronouncing place names is not as easy as it may look. The Malagasy alphabet has 21 letters, and many syllables are often dropped when speaking, e.g. 'Ranomafana' is pronounced 'Ran'mafaan'. 'A' is pronounced long, as in bar, e.g. Ambanja is pronounced 'Ambaandz'. 'E' is pronounced as in get, e.g. Betroka is pronounced 'Betrook'. 'I' as in bin, e.g. Ambohitantely, pronounced 'Amboohitantel'. 'O' as in too, e.g. Ambositra is pronounced 'Amboostr'. 'S' becomes a silent 'sh', e.g. Isalo is 'Ishaal'. 'J' becomes 'dz', e.g. as in Mahajanga, which becomes 'Mahadzanga'.

vast number of secondary gods or nature spirits which inhabit certain trees, rocks or rivers. These spirits can influence the lives of people, who may then visit sites to pray to the spirits reportedly residing there. Spirits can also possess humans, sending them into trances (an important and regular phenomenon in some tribes). Spirits are also said to inhabit certain animals, particularly crocodiles.

Burial Practices

Tombs are regarded by Malagasy as permanent homes, while the houses of the living are only temporary. Thus time, money and effort is spent improving the tombs as an investment for the future. After a death in the family, a ritual known as *sasa* is performed. The living relatives go to a fast-flowing river with all their clothes (including the garments they are wearing on their backs), which are then washed to rid them of any impurities. Zebu are sacrificed as a gesture of respect. In other places, such as among the Antaisaka tribe, the ceremony involves glueing money onto the corpse.

Not everyone is entitled to a tomb or burial. Sorcerers are dumped to the west of their villages and barely covered with soil, so that their bodies can be eaten by feral dogs and other animals. Their necks are twisted so that their heads face to the south. Also, in the Antaisaka tribe, twins were usually killed or abandoned in the forest after birth. Today this is against the law but twins may still not be buried in tombs.

Fady

The Malagasy follow a vast, complex system of beliefs pertaining to all aspects of everyday life. These vary from village to village and even family to family. *Fady* are not taboos, as is popularly believed, but beliefs related to actions, objects or social events. There are three categories of *fady*: those related to actions, for example, believing it is *fady* to sing while you are eating and if you do, you will develop elongated teeth; those related to objects, particularly food; and *fady* related to social events – for example, the Merina will not have funerals on Tuesdays as this may bring about another death in the family. In many areas it is considered *fady* to point at

Fady and Etiquette

Some examples of *fady* found around Madagascar are:

- Access to **burial sites** is forbidden unless accompanied by a local guide.
- Avoid disturbing the trees, stones or rivers regarded locally as **sacred** (e.g. don't swim in a sacred pool or enter an *ala fady*).
- **Pregnant Sakalava women** may not sit in open doorways – they represent the birth canal and sitting in them may result in complications during childbirth.
- During a wake, do not make noise after **midnight**, otherwise **witches** will know someone has died and will go to the tomb and attempt to block the soul's flight to the *razana*.
- If visiting **Ambohimanga**, enter with your right foot first and leave with your left foot first.
- Among the **Betsileo**, tenrecs are *fady* and cannot be eaten or kept in captivity.
- In eastern regions, **never** use a door on the **east-facing** side of a house. It is used solely for taking the dead out of the house.

▶ *Right: Antandroy musicians in the south.*
▶▶ *Opposite: Sakalava woman wearing a lamba, the popular wraparound.*

The Red Shoes

Paddy Bush, an associate of the Anglo-Malagasy Society, Madagascar music expert and brother of acclaimed British musician Kate Bush, has undertaken a number of extensive journeys around Madagascar. Most recently, Bush accompanied and co-presented an astonishing series of six programmes for BBC radio on the music of Madagascar. This included a spine-tingling recording of a Hira Gasy. Bush mastered playing the *valiha* and *marovany*, and presented the superb documentary *Like A God When He Plays,* during which he attended the *famadihana* (bone-turning ceremony) of the musical legend Rakotozafy near Lac Alaotra. Also featuring was Madagascar's musical ambassador, Justin Vali, whose album *The Sunshine Within* was produced by Paddy Bush. On Kate Bush's album *The Red Shoes,* Malagasy influence by her brother and Justin Vali is prominent in various tracks. Part of the album – which brought Malagasy music to the attention of a wider audience – has been remixed and is to be released in 2011. For Malagasy music updates, *see* www.madagate.com

tombs. Foreigners are usually exempt from having to adhere to *fady*, but it is considerate to find out as much as possible about this in regions you are visiting so as to avoid offending local people.

Ody and *Fanafody*

Ody are fetishes and *fanafody* herbal medicines or remedies. About 60% of Madagascar's vast array of plants (over 8500 have been catalogued to date, with the total estimated to be 12,000) have medicinal properties. There are three categories of *ody*: collective fetishes, for example, a sacred stone, proclaimed as such by a chief or other high-ranking member of the community; individual fetishes, amulets or objects used just by one person; and talismans.

Ody can also be used in a destructive manner, for example, by thieves who want to succeed in crime. They can also be used in black magic, for example, to gain someone's love. Sorcerers sell various *ody* for negative purposes, in exchange for money, zebu or poultry. A red rooster is preferred. Only with Christianity was the concept of hell (*helo*) introduced to the Malagasy.

Music

'The Malagasy have a musical culture that is as fantastic and unique as their wildlife' (Paddy Bush, music instrument technologist, producer and critic, 2005).

Traditionally most accomplished Malagasy vocalists are from the south and instrumentalists from the highlands. The two elements have sometimes blended to create captivating music. Most Malagasy music is lively, and in coastal areas, the African influence is apparent.

The national instrument is the *valiha,* a family of box or bamboo pole zithers with up to 28 strings and frets around it. The *valiha* does not have any semitones and sounds somewhat like a harp. Since the 1940s, a handful of families – notably the Rakotondrasoa family of renowned *valiha* virtuoso Justin Vali – have been responsible for making almost all *valihas* for the highlands. *Valiha* resemble similar instruments in southeastern Asia. According to the leading expert on Malagasy music, Paddy Bush, the Asian bamboo zithers are used to appease the animistic forest spirits during possession ceremonies. The *kabosy* is a guitar that resembles a banjo and the *jejolava* is a single-stringed instrument which is used together with a gourd. There are various flutes, including the *kiloloka,* on which only one note can be played; so to create a chord, a few flautists must play simultaneously. French influence is reflected in accordions and clarinets.

The most internationally recognized Malagasy musician is Justin Vali. Within Madagascar, however, other dynamic musicians such as D'Gary and Jojoby have large following. Salala's music is more focused on harmonies and traditional sounds, and the music of Mahaleo contains profound lyrical content. Look for posters displayed in the larger towns which advertise live shows, or enquire at your hotel reception. The *Donia* of Nosy Bé is one of a number of annual music festivals held in Madagascar.

Malagasy Dress

A conspicuous element in traditional Malagasy clothing is the *lamba,* a wrapround sheet often printed with designs depicting

Useful Words

trano • house
be • big
ve / kely • small
manga • blue
rano • water
vary • rice
atody • eggs
moto • bread
lalana • road
tanana • town
ony • river
omby • ox
zaza • child
lava • tall / long
nosy • island
lehilahy / vehivavy • man / woman
maro • many
mangatsika • its cold
yoh / tsia • yes / no
ohatrinona? • how much?
aiza? • where is?
misy ve? • is there any...
mila... aho • I want...

Popular Malagasy Recipes

Coconut chicken: This is a popular dish on Madagascar. To make the coconut milk, mix one grated coconut with a cup of hot water. Push through a sieve. Bring mixture close to boiling point. Fry chicken portions in oil, add diced onion and tomatoes, saffron, garlic and ground ginger. Add a pinch of pepper and a cup of flour to the coconut milk. Pour milk over chicken when cooked.

Cinnamon Rum: Boil cinnamon sticks in rum. Add vanilla pods and some sugar. Stir the mixture until it becomes a syrup. Dilute with rum and leave to mature for at least a month.

Chicken with garlic and ginger (Akoho misy Sakamalao): Grate a 5cm (2in) piece fresh ginger, crush 6 garlic cloves, add salt to taste and mix together in a small bowl. Rub this mixture all over 4 large chicken joints, halved. Heat 2 tbsp oil in a large frying pan, add the seasoned chicken and cook gently over a low heat for about 40 minutes, turning from time to time, until the chicken is cooked through. Serve hot.

everyday scenes. Some cheaper *lambas* also have slogans on them which should be checked before the cloth is paid for – some can be really suggestive. In the highlands, particularly among the Betsileo people, *lambas* are worn on the shoulder. If it trails off to the person's right, it symbolizes mourning. *Lamba mena* (red lambas) are reserved for special occasions and are also used as burial shrouds.

The other noticeable element in Malagasy dress is the straw hat. These vary regionally, from broad-brimmed hats to brimless, tight-fitting, cone-shaped hats that can be seen in the south and central west. Western influence is increasingly apparent and fashion (especially in urban areas like Tana) tends to follow trends set by fashion magazines such as *Elle* and *Vogue*. There is therefore a huge demand for trainers, jeans and leather jackets.

Sport and Recreation

Football is especially popular in Madagascar, as is evidenced by football fields in just about every town. Volleyball and basketball have taken off too. The popularity of martial arts mushroomed after Bruce Lee movies were screened in Madagascar. Young people enjoy foosball, or table football, while local board games include *fanora*, which resembles draughts but is more complex, and *katra*, a simpler game aimed at collecting piles of

▶ *Right: Strings of colourful vakana beads above traditional remedies* (fanafody). *Healers or* Ombiasy *suggest combinations of these beads to customers, depending on the nature of their situation.*

stones on a board. As tourism increases more centres are established for equestrian sports, water sports, golf and tennis.

▲ *Above: Spicy stews, rice and baguettes are the standard fare in most of the hotels.*

Food and Drink

Foodies are sure to enjoy munching their way around Madagascar, savouring the fusion cuisine with its French and Indonesian influences. In hotels, international fare is readily available but do try local dishes where you can. Usually they come with generous servings of the Malagasy staple, rice (*vary*), accompanied by a stew (*brede*), vegetables (*legumes*) and one or more of the following meats: *henan-omby* or beef (zebu – ask for it well done if having a steak); *henan-akoho* or chicken; *henan-kisoa* or pork; and *henan drano* or fish. A tasty dish combining pork and manioc leaves is known as *ravitoto*.

The national dish is a meat and vegetable casserole called *romazava*, with the national desert, *banane flambé*, following afterwards. This is a peeled banana with white rum poured over it and set alight. (Watch your hair!) Cheese is excellent, as is butter, yet milk is hardly seen. Excellent quality fruit is abundant. In season, from November to February, lychees are the speciality of the east and mangoes of the west. In winter, citrus from the highlands is usually on offer.

Local wines, rums and beers are plentiful and cheap. 'Fresh' (a bottled beer shandy) is excellent after a day out in the forests. Cold drinks are freely available. Bottled mineral water is also readily obtained all over Madagascar. Look out for fermented sugar-cane juice (*betsabetsa*), fermented coconut milk (*trembo*) and *punch au coco* (rum with coconut milk).

Madagascar's Wines

The area around Fianarantsoa and Ambalavao has some 2000ha (4942 acres) of vineyards, first introduced onto the island by Jean Laborde and then by the Swiss in the 1970s. Most of the grapes are used for the locally produced range of wines. Best known of the wine estates is Lazan'i Betsileo, the wines of which are sold all over Madagascar. Recent tastings have reported the rosé and dry white to be good, and the red wine somewhat less so.

安全生产

2. Antananarivo and the Highlands

Antananarivo, the lively Malagasy **capital** city, is set in a basin surrounded by 12 sacred hills, at about 1250m (4101ft) above sea level. The city retains a picture-book beauty about it, with cobbled streets winding their way among narrow two- or three-storey buildings. On the outskirts, wherever space permit, are soft green rice paddies with houses of red brick and wood set on little islets.

Much of the **old-world charm** of Antananarivo (or **Tana**, as it is abbreviated) derives from its architecture, which is mainly of French origin. It is interspersed with elements from other parts of Europe, one of the more obvious being the Victorian English influence in the houses' carved balconies. **Ox carts** still move slowly along its streets and many of the motor vehicles date back to the 1970s and '80s. Some are in a delightful state of disrepair as spare parts are in short supply. There are still few bland and modern skyscrapers.

Tana is the centre of the **Merina**, one of the most numerous of Madagascar's dominant ethnic groups or 'tribes', as the Malagasy refer to themselves. It is the Merina who have the most recognizable connection with the original Malayo-Polynesian component of the Malagasy forebears.

The capital has excellent hotels and restaurants, galleries and museums, markets, shops, and plenty to see for those with an interest in **culture**, **architecture** and **history**. The central location means it functions as a 'hub' on most Madagascar itineraries.

Don't Miss

*** **Ranomafana National Park:** wildlife galore in spectacular rainforest.

** **Antsirabe** and **Ambositra:** for craft workshops and picturesque highlands scenery.

** **Ambalavao**, **Andringitra** and **Anjaha:** dramatic landscapes and iconic ring-tailed lemurs.

** A **ride** from **Fianarantsoa** to **Sahambavy** on the world's only Micheline.

◀ *Opposite: Panoramic view over Lac Anosy in Antananarivo.*

Climate

The highlands can be visited all year round. Summer days are pleasantly hot and winter nights can be crisp to very cold. Rains fall mostly from November to April. In the rainy months you will probably experience brief, scattered thundershowers, punctuated by hours of blazing sunshine. On the eastern escarpment (Anjozorobe, Ranomafana), however, rainfall is much higher.

ANTANANARIVO

Most visitors flying to the country still land at Tana's Ivato Airport, and the drive from there to the city shows off a variety of small **trading stores**, ***hotelys*** (bars-cum-eateries), houses bordered by rice paddies, and increasingly **modern supermarkets** and **shopping centres**. Approaching the city centre there are numerous impressive colonial buildings, many of which stand on fairly steep hillsides. In the surrounding countryside are intriguing little hamlets and the solid **Merina tombs** in which the departed are interred. Although there has been substantial development during the last 15 years, visiting Tana is happily still somewhat like entering a hazy time warp. By day and night the city is a hive of activity: everyone appears engaged in making, doing and selling things.

Central Tana

Analakely in 'lower town' was until the cleanup campaign in the 1990s home of one of the world's biggest open-air markets. (The name of the market, *Zoma*, means 'Friday' in Malagasy.) At the Zoma – as is the case now in the existing markets – people sold everything imaginable. Unfortunately the central area of Avenue de l'Indépendance and Avenue du 26 Juin 1960, and its intriguing labyrinth of side streets, was never really particularly safe for tourists and it is best avoided, particularly at night. In the **Artisans' Markets**, on the other hand, you will find security guards.

▲ *Above: Rice paddies are established wherever space permits around Antananarivo.*

The large lake in Tana is **Lac Anosy**, which looks really lovely when the surrounding jacarandas are in flower in October and November. In the middle of the lake is a monument erected by the French to the casualties of World War I.

Upper Town and the Rova

Separating Analakely from **Haute-Ville** or 'upper town' is a steep flight of stairs. The queen's palace, the **Rova**, is situated on the highest hill overlooking Tana and is undergoing restoration following a sensless fire in 1995, which caused severe damage.

The original queen's palace, **Manjakamiadama** (meaning 'where it is pleasant to reign from'), was built out of wood in 1839 for Queen Ranavalona I by Jean Laborde. This construction was shielded by a stone structure built by James Cameron, a Scottish missionary and architect.

Near the Rova was a simpler, narrow dwelling which once belonged to King Andrianampoinimerina, who united Madagascar at the end of the 18th century and proclaimed Tana as his capital. His palace is at the UNESCO World Heritage Cultural Site of **Ambohimanga**, a royal village that can be seen from the Rova. Two additional wooden buildings in the royal compound, the **Tranomanara**, enclosed royal tombs containing the remains of four queens and three kings.

The bronze eagle statue at the Rova entrance honours the *voromaheny*, or 'eagles', King Radama I's troops. Other buildings in the compound included the Silver Palace (Tranavola), also designed by Jean Laborde for Queen Ranavalona I, and Manampisoa, built for Queen Rasoherina in 1866 by William Poole, a British missionary. Items of interest in Manampisoa included gifts and letters from British monarchs and Napoleon III.

The rock cliffs nearby are known as Ampamarinana, 'the place of the hurling', off which Christians were thrown during the reign of Queen Ranavalona.

Best Buys

Here are just a few items to look for in the markets and craft shops:
- zebu leather belts and handbags.
- colourful *lambas* featuring scenes of everyday life.
- wooden carvings, including replicas of the totems/stelae.
- solitaire sets with semi-precious gemstone spheres.
- intricately embroidered tablecloths and clothing.
- Antaimoro paper for wall-hangings, lampshades or elegant stationery.
- Malagasy chocolates, coffee and vanilla – all excellent!
- Model cars or rickshaws ingeniously crafted from discarded tins.

Tana's Street Kids

There are inspiring programmes in Tana to help the poorest families. Centre Fihavanana (run by the Sisters of the Good Shepherd, 58 Lalana S. Stephani, Amparibe, tel: 22 29981, e-mail: bpfihavanana@moov.mg) offers education, training and meals, assisting some 300 street children aged 3–12, providing education, training and work for destitute mothers and elderly people and also bicycles for unemployed young men. Visiting the centre is a humbling experience. The children's home Akany Avoko (tel: 22 44158, e-mail: akany-avoko@wanadoo.mg) provides food, clothing, education and shelter to about 150 homeless children, disabled children and teenage mothers. To send a donation from abroad, contact the Welsh charity 'Money For Madagascar' (info@moneyformadagascar.org) which supports agricultural and health projects, as well as destitute urban people in both centres. *See* www.moneyformadagascar.org

Tsimbazaza Zoo, Botanical Gardens and Museum ★

Set in extensive park-like surroundings that include a lake with a large heronry, Tsimbazaza is about 4km (2.5 miles) from the city centre.

The **zoo** has seen structural improvement under organizations such as the Madagascar Fauna Group, and now holds a fair selection of **lemurs**, including **aye ayes** in their nocturnal animal house – to visit them you need a permit that must be arranged in advance through a tour operator.

The **reptile house** is a modern, solid and clean structure displaying a variety of endemic reptiles, frogs and mammals. In the aviaries various endemic birds are housed.

The **Museum of Ethnology and Paleontology** is worth a visit, especially for the elephant bird skeleton and egg, and those of some extinct giant lemurs.

The **Botanical Gardens** has a growing selection of Malagasy plants, selected primarily by the exemplary NGO Missouri Botanical Gardens (MBG), which has long been active in Madagascar. Wandering around the grounds you may encounter a variety of small **wildlife** too, including snakes, chameleons and birds.

AROUND ANTANANARIVO

Ambohimanga ★★★

The site of the Merina monarchs' summer houses, the royal village of Ambohimanga is 21km (13 miles) from Tana by road and makes for a popular and leisurely half-day excursion. There are elegant gardens, a restaurant, and wide, panoramic views over the surrounding Imerina.

Lake Mantasoa ★

About 60km (37 miles) east of Antananarivo, the man-made lake of Mantasoa is where Jean Laborde built a summer home for Queen Ranavalona I, as well as a

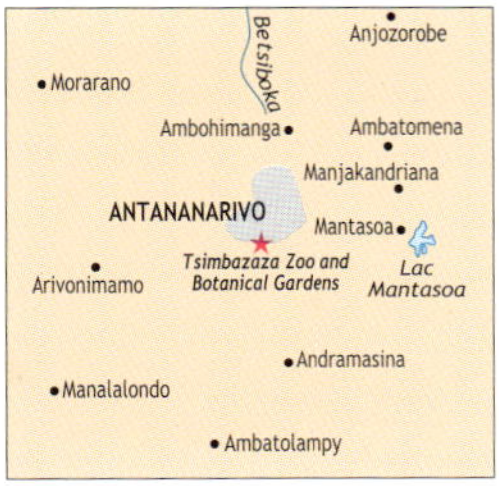

factory to manufacture weaponry for the Merina monarchy. Because forced labour was used for these achievements, the workers exacted their revenge by rebelling and destroying much of the site in the 19th century. The Domain de l'Ermitage Hotel is used as a weekend retreat by wealthy residents of Antananarivo and offers **tennis**, **riding**, **boating** and **walking trails**.

Anjozorobe **

Part of an extensive forest corridor, Anjozorobe is one of the last remaining tracts of rainforest on the High Plateau. The drive from Antananarivo is about two hours to the northeast, and there is accommodation at the excellent Mananara Lodge and Saha Forest Camp. Although nine species of lemur are present, they are wary and very hard to see at present. For naturalists interested in birds and reptiles the site can be very rewarding, provided you are accompanied by a knowledgeable, professional guide. Night walks may reveal various chameleons and leaf-tailed geckoes.

ANTSIRABE TO FIANARANTSOA

The RN7 (Route Nationale 7) road from Tana to the southwestern coastal town of Tuléar is the most popular overland route in Madagascar, with good reason. Scenery along the

Anjozorobe

This 2500ha (6177-acre) montane rainforest in the Anjozorobe-Angavo corridor is managed by the NGO, FANAMBY. Two hours' drive northeast of Tana, it is rewarding for birding and for 'herping' (particularly chameleons and geckoes). There are nine lemurs (not yet well habituated). There is a network of trails and mountain bike tracks. To get the most out of your visit, travel with an experienced, Antananarivo-based naturalist guide. Mananara Lodge and Saha Forest Camp provide accommodation. Anjozorobe is a known site for two of Madagascar's rarest endemic wetland birds, the Meller's Duck and the Slender-billed Flufftail, so is popular with the international birding fraternity. *See* www.fanamby.org.mg

▲ Above: The Madagascar comet moth is much larger than its African relative.
◀ Opposite: The aye aye epitomizes bizarre Malagasy fauna. It can be seen at the national zoo where it's part of an international breeding programme.

Ialatsara Lemur Park

About 65km (40 miles) north of Fianar on the RN7, this relatively recently opened private reserve contains 1000ha (2471 acres) of eastern rainforest and a larger area of plantation. Facilities consist of seven basic wood-frame and canvas rooms on platforms, with comfortable beds and communal facilities. Among the prolific wildlife is the strikingly attractive Milne-Edwards diadem sifaka. Walks are graded from easy to fairly demanding.

way includes terraced highlands, dense rainforest, dramatic granite outcrops and sandstone mountains, and culminates in the sub-arid south. The road is now fully paved.

Antsirabe ★★

At an altitude of 1500m (4900ft), the first large town 169km (105 miles) south of Tana enjoys a refreshing, almost temperate climate. The broad avenue that ends in front of the station is usually buzzing with colourful *pousse-pousse* (rickshaws), and this mode of transport is the very best way in which to explore the interesting craft shops for which Antsirabe is well known. It is also an important industrial centre, mainly for its beer breweries and dairy factories.

Many visitors make an excursion to the volcanic lake **Tritriva**, west of town. Tritriva's waters are surrounded by steep cliffs and fringed by a pine plantation and the water level rises in the dry season. Swimming is risky due to peculiar currents, probably caused by lava tubes. Peregrine falcons nest in the rock faces.

Ambositra ★★

The next large town on the road from Tana to Tuléar, Ambositra is 95km (59 miles) south of Antsirabe, a drive of about two hours. The highlands scenery along the way is quite spectacular, with the road winding around hills and passing through valleys. Ambositra is best known as a centre for wooden craftwork and there are many different workshops to choose from. Most visitors stop only for a few hours on their way between Fianarantsoa and Antsirabe. *Savika*, or bull-fighting, is held in large arenas here.

▼ Below: The picturesque Betsileo centre of Fianarantsoa is known for its vineyards, tea estates and terraced rice fields.

Fianarantsoa ★

The name of Madagascar's second city means 'place of learning'. Centre of the Betsileo tribe, Fianar is two hours south of Ambositra along the RN7. It constitutes one of Madagascar's most densely populated regions. The city is split into three sections: upper town (**Haute-Ville**) is pleasant, with impressive colonial buildings and churches, while lower town (**Basse-Ville**) is somewhat decayed. In the middle level (**Nouvelle-Ville**) are banks and business centres. An impressive market is held on Fridays.

An enjoyable excursion which can be arranged here is a 45-minute ride on the world's only remaining Micheline to the Sahambavy area, about 25km (15.5 miles) to the east. Here you can visit a tea estate and relax at the simple Lac Hotel in picturesque surrounds.

RANOMAFANA NATIONAL PARK ★★★

Cut by the tumbling whitewater **Namorona River**, this 41,600ha (102,793-acre) national park is one of Madagascar's best-known rainforest wildlife hot spots. The park was gazetted in 1991 following the discovery in 1986 of the **golden bamboo lemur** by primatologists Patricia Wright and Bernard Meier.

Like most of the other rainforest parks, Ranomafana consists largely of steep, forested slopes over which there are **well-designed trails**. Some lead up to lookout points from where views are mesmerizing. The trails are fairly demanding and most take a few hours. Leeches are common in this park, but, fortunately for walkers, they are tiny compared to those that are found on the continents. There is currently only one good lodge servicing the park.

In addition to protecting the golden bamboo lemur, Ranomafana holds 11 other species of **lemur**, including the greater (broad-nosed) bamboo lemur, which was rediscovered here after having gone AWOL for almost a century. During a rainforest walk it is not difficult to see four or five lemur species, including red-fronted brown lemur, red-bellied lemur, eastern grey bamboo lemur and black-and-white ruffed lemur. Along with Ialatsara, it is the best place in which to see the striking **Milne-Edward's**

Saving Ranomafana

Thanks largely to the continued efforts of Dr Patricia Wright, Ranomafana remains a high-profile national park. Achievements have been manifold: park guides have been trained, a museum and information centre opened and employment has been created for local residents. There some 65 research technicians and 50 guides employed, plus park rangers. Hotels and stalls or shops create more job opportunities. Conservation committees were established in the villages, educational programmes set up to improve agricultural techniques, reforestation was started, schools opened and a clinic built. Dr Wright, who leads teams of students (and also interested non-academics) into the park annually to learn about the conservation successes and also failures, puts the programme's success down to transparency.

In December 2011 the Institute for Conservation of Tropical Environments and MICET in Madagascar are opening the Centre ValBio campus. Dr Wright emphasises a current need for outreach in conservation education and health issues.

For more information, contact micet@moov.mg or icte.information@gmail.com

▲ *Above: The eastern ring-tailed mongoose is one of the most attractive of Madagascar's endemic carnivores and is easily seen in Ranomafana.*

diadem sifaka, with its piercing ruby-red eyes. Nocturnal lemurs include the eastern avahi, small-toothed sportive lemur, greater dwarf lemur and rufous mouse lemur.

Unfortunately, night walks are currently prohibited in any state-run parks or reserves. Guides will, however, arrange these outside the park's perimeter.

Other mammals present include the hyperkinetic and diurnal eastern ring-tailed mongoose. Common tenrecs are often seen, sometimes followed by a gang of yellow-and-black-streaked youngsters.

Ranomafana is woven into all **birding** itineraries, with a list of some 118 species recorded here. The ultra-elusive slender-billed flufftail, one of the island's rarest and most enigmatic birds, was rediscovered here by ornithologist Lucienne Wilmé. Other highlights include brown mesite, velvet and sunbird asitys, and the lovely pitta-like ground-roller. Birders also visit Vohiparara to seek species which prefer higher altitudes.

You may see some unusual-looking reptiles such as the leaf-mimicking, satanic leaf-tailed gecko and also invertebrates like the enormous Malagasy comet, or lunar moth. The area is also known for its colourful profusion of **orchids**.

Time for Tea

High-quality tea is produced on the eastern escarpment, especially around Fianarantsoa. An accessible estate, Sahambavy, is about 25km (15 miles) from Fianar, in the direction of Manakara. Most of the tea it produces is for export. Some enjoy getting there by train, or contact Za Tour, the only Malagasy tour operator who offers excursions on the world's sole operational Micheline. Za Tour recommends combining a visit to Sahambavy with lunch at the Tsara Guest House in Fianarantsoa, after which they can take you to Ranomafana; tel: 22 42286, zatour@iris.mg www.zatours-madagascar.com

FIANARANTSOA TO IHOSY

Ambalavao ★★

For those heading south from Fianarantsoa, the next large town is Ambalavao, 56km (35 miles) further along the RN7. As in many highlands settlements, houses have wooden balconies, carved railings and tiled roofs. There is an **Antaimoro paper** factory, a cattle market and a winery here. The exquisite Antaimoro paper is made from sisal pulp, into which colourful flowers are pressed.

Continuing southwards, you will enter a landscape dominated by enormous granite domes or inselbergs. About 17km (10.5 miles) south of Ambalavao is the small, locally run **Anjaha Community Conservation Site**. Here you can see robust and well-habituated ring-tailed lemurs thriving in spectacular surrounds with some interesting flora.

Some spectacular **photographic opportunities** exist along this road, including the intricately terraced hillsides, which support rice crops. Vineyards and some massive inselbergs, which rise abruptly from flat, grass-covered plains, can also be seen along the way.

Andringitra National Park ★★★

Back in 1927 a substantial section of this imposing **granitic range** was granted legal protection. The 310km^2 (120-sq-mile) national park is about 50km (31 miles) south of Ambalavao. Madagascar's second highest mountain, **Pic Imarivolanitra** ('Pic Boby', 2658m/8721ft), is here. This is also where the lowest temperature in the country was recorded (-8°C/18°F in June 1980). The landscape includes massive granite formations, waterfalls and steep cliffs. There are **forests**, **grasslands** and **moorlands**, and in spring and summer, delightful **wild flower** displays. **Wildlife** is varied but not habituated, so the area is visited mostly by

▶ *Right: Zebu ox carts are the most commonly used mode of transport in rural Madagascar. This one, made from an old Renault, was photographed near Ihosy.*

adventure travellers who come to do trekking, rock climbing and paragliding outside the park. Antananarivo-based tour operator Boogie Pilgrim has a permanent tented camp, **Tsara Camp**, outside the park (about 40km/25 miles south of Ambalavao) and are able to arrange various adventure activities. Experienced trekking enthusiasts can take on one of the four thoughtfully created **trails** in the park, such as the Diavalona trail, which takes up to a day to complete.

Highlights of the RN7

- Marvellous **tombs** at various places along the way – Merina tombs at Ambatolampy, Mahafaly, and Masikoro tombs at Andranovory.
- Changing **architecture**, from intricately designed highland homes of the Merina and Betsileo to simple Bara houses and the rural dwellings of the Veso and Antandroy.
- **Scenery:** highlands, rice paddies, vineyards (terraced in Bestileo country), rainforest (Ranomafana), inselbergs (Ambalavao), spiny desert, sea and beaches.
- **Wildlife** at Ialatsara, Ranomafana, Andringitra, Anjaha, Isalo, Zombitse and Ifaty.
- **Shopping:** local shops sell various items (crafts especially) you may not find in Tana.
- **Hiking trails** at Ranomafana, Andringitra and Isalo.

Ihosy

Travelling from Ambalavao towards Ihosy, you pass the **Varavarana ny Atsimo** ('door to the south') – two enormous rock formations – and find yourself in the desolate outback which is the land of the **Bara**. The change in architecture is abrupt and fascinating: the Bara still build square homes, but of a much simpler design than the houses of the highlands people. Cassava and maize fields replace rice paddies. Ihosy is a centre of the Bara (thought to be one of the younger Malagasy tribes), a dark-skinned people with marked African features who prize cattle and place little value on other material possessions. Young men still have to prove their manhood by thieving some cattle. Continuing along the RN7 route, you then reach the eerily silent **Horombe Plateau**, dotted with the fire-resistant Bismarkia palms. Ranohira, the access town to the sandstone mountain national park of Isalo, is 91km (56.5 miles) from Ihosy.

BEST TIMES TO VISIT

Tana and the Highlands can be visited **year round**. In winter (June, July and August), mornings and evenings are cold, and in summer the weather is generally hot and slightly **humid**. From October to February heavy storms may occur suddenly, causing frequent but short power cuts in smaller hotels. **Winter** nights are cool to very cold, especially in the escarpment and mountains.

GETTING THERE

Air Madagascar (tel: 22 22 2222, www.airmadagascar.com) operates flights to Antananarivo from Paris CDG, Milan, Johannesburg, Mauritius and Nairobi. If flying internationally with the national carrier, you can benefit from discounts on domestic flights.

Air France (tel: 23 23001/23, www.airfrance.com) also operates regular flights from Paris CDG to Antananarivo.

Corsair (www.corsairfly.com) is another alternative, either direct from Paris or via Réunion in conjunction with **Air Austral** (call centre tel: +33 825 013 012, www.air-austral.com).

SA Airlink (tel: +27 11 987 1111, www.saairlink.co.za) operates several flights weekly between Johannesburg and Antananarivo. For the best prices on SA Airlink, which also has a small allocation of seats on many Air Madagascar domestic flights, be sure to book early.

Air Mauritius (tel: +230 207 7575, www.airmauritius.com) operates flights from Mauritius to Antananarivo. For families it is an ideal choice, if flying from the UK, as the journey back can be broken with a stay in Mauritius.

Kenya Airways (www.kenya-airways.com) operates several flights per week between Nairobi and Antananarivo. It competes with Air France as the most utilized carrier for visitors from the UK.

Ivato Antananarivo Airport is about 30–45 minutes' drive from Tana town centre, depending on traffic.

GETTING AROUND

For those without pre-arranged transportation, taxis are widely available in most urban centres and they represent good value for money. Useful when you have days at leisure and no set schedule to adhere to. For adventurous, independent travellers who understand some French, there are the infamous *taxi brousse* (bush taxis). They tend to leave taxi ranks from 06:00–08:00 but this is wholly dependent on when the vehicle is packed to capacity.

Rickshaws (*pousse-pousse/posy-posy*) are a fun way to get around in many urban centres.

The simplest way to get around Madagascar is to pre-arrange your trip through a reputable tour operator or travel agent. This allows you to make the most of your time in a country with a difficult geography and modest infrastructure.

WHERE TO STAY

Antananarivo

LUXURY

Colbert Carayon, Annex of the Colbert, Rue Printsy Ratsimamanga, Antaninenarina, tel: 22 20202, www.colbert-hotel.com Impressive and opulent.

Royal Palissandre Hotel & Spa, 13 Rue Andriandahifotsy-Faravohitra, tel: 22 60560, hotelpalissandre@simicro.mg www.hotel-palissandre.com On a hillside overlooking Tana, this charming hotel has a spa, and the restaurant serves Malagasy and international cuisine.

Carlton Madagascar, Rue Pierre Stibbe Anosy, Antananarivo 101, Antananarivo, tel: 22 26060, contact@carlton.mg www.carlton-madagascar.com Good for business people, with 171 rooms, including 6 suites, 7 non-smoking floors and one room for disabled guests.

MID-RANGE

La Varangue, 17 Rue Printsy Ratsimamanga, Antaninenarina, tel: 22 27397, varangue@simicro.mg Creole-style building with views from terrace. Rooms have safe, TV and mini-bar. Outstanding food.

Residence Lapasoa, 15 Rue de la Réunion, Isoraka, tel: 22 61140, corossol@malagasy.com www.lapasoa.com Ten comfortable rooms in tastefully renovated colonial villa. Internet access, and the popular and trendy restaurant KuDeTa.

Lokanga, tel: 22 235 44, contact@lokangahotel-mg www.lokanga-hotel.mg With great views of the capital and only six rooms, this beautifully decorated establishment is currently the accommodation of choice for those after a small boutique hotel in Antananarivo. Excellent food. Highly recommended.

Tamboho Hotel, tel: 22 69300, resa@hoteltamboho.com Near a shopping centre. Excellent restaurant, heated pool and spa. WiFi connection. Highly recommended.

Near Ivato Airport

Le Relais des Plateaux, tel: 22 44122, mobile: 032 05 678 93, www.relais-des-plateaux.com A 5–10 minute drive from Ivato airport. Neat rooms, recently refurbished, with large restaurant built around a pool. The restaurant receives very favourable feedback.

Anjozorobe

Mananara Lodge, tel: 22 53070, mananaralodge@boogiepilgrim-madagascar.com www.mananaralodge-madagascar.com Permanent tented camp: spacious tents on wooden platforms under thatch, spacious bathrooms, and a dining tent with a lounge. Popular with birders and hikers.

Saha Forest Camp: the NGO FANAMBY has done a commendable job with the establishment of this eco-lodge: a collection of comfortable wooden chalets, beautifully appointed, near the rainforest. Guests can visit Antsahabe village for a cultural experience. Book through tour operators, e.g. Za Tours, zatour@iris.mg

Antsirabe

Luxury

Couleur Café, Route Ambositra, Antsirabe, tel: 032 02 20065, www.couleurcafeantsirabe.com A non-smoking hotel, with 4 comfortable *en-suite* 'pavillion' rooms and a family villa with two rooms, in spacious gardens. Now the hotel of choice in Antsirabe.

Mid-range

La Residence Camelia, tel: 44 48844, camellia@simicro.mg www.laresidencecamelia.com Suitable alternative to Couleur Café. Extras are expensive.

Ambositra

L'Artisan, tel: 034 04 64253, 033 04 56697, 032 51 99609, artisan_hôtel@yahoo.fr Good accommodation in Ambositra. Beautifully decorated, the main building is a traditional Merina-styled house with a restaurant. Bungalows are scattered in a lovely garden.

Fianarantsoa

Luxury

Tsara Guesthouse, BP 1373, Fianarantsoa 301, tel: 75 502 06, www.tsaraguest.com Has 16 rooms; great views from the terrace; excellent restaurant. The English-speaking owner offers a range of excursions.

Mid-range

Zomatel, Place du Zoma, BP1367, Fianarantsoa, 301, tel: 2075 50797, resa@zomatel.com www.zomatel-madagascar.com Fifty-two spacious rooms, so can cater for small tour groups. Clean, well maintained, has a pool, and is suitable as overnight stop on the RN7 route.

Ranomafana National Park

Setam Lodge, tel: 24 31071/22, setamlodge@wanadoo.mg The best – and at times the only option worth considering in Ranomafana, the lodge is 1km from the park entrance. Limited menu. Lovely view of the rainforest. Book long in advance.

Where to Eat

Antananarivo

Luxury

Restaurant Tranovola, Route d'Ambohipo, tel: 22 33471. Wonderful Malagasy cuisine. Live traditional music.

MID-RANGE
La Table d'Hôte de Mariette, 11 Rue Georges V, Fahavohitra, tel: 22 21602.
Le Grille du Rova, tel: 22 62724. Near the Rova. Highly recommended.
Akany Avoko Café, tel: 22 44158. Organic meals.

Antsirabe
MID-RANGE
L'Arche Restaurant, tel: 032 027 4925027. French-owned with cosy atmosphere and fine food.

Fianarantsoa
MID-RANGE
Restaurant Le Panda, Rue Printsy Ramaharo, tel: 75 50569. Serves good Chinese food.

TOURS AND EXCURSIONS

Antananarivo and Environs
Za Tours (tel: 20 24 25307/8 or 20 22 42286, www.zatour-madagascar.com).
Madagascar National Tourist Office, Lot IBG 29C Antsahavola, tel: 20 22 66115, www.madagascar-tourisme.com Consult your tour operator to arrange activities safely.
ORTANA (Regional Tourism Office). Located at the base of the stairway leading to Ave de l'Indépendance, tel: 24 30484, www.tourisme-antananarivo.com Open Monday–Friday 08:30–17:00, Saturday 08:00–16:00.
Museum of Art and Archaeology, 17 Rue Dr Villette, Isoraka (near Residence Lapasoa).

Fianarantsoa
Tsara Guesthouse, tel: 75 502 06, tsaraguest@wanadoo.mg Offers excursions. Book well in advance.

SHOPPING

Artisans Market, Route Digue, District 67, Mon 09:00–17:00. Malagasy handicrafts.
BioAroma, 54 Ave General Ramanantsoa, tel: 22 32630. Health and beauty products, massages.
Centre Fihavanana, run by the Sisters Of The Good Shepherd in Mahamasina (most of the nuns speak English). Handicrafts. *See* the Money for Madagascar website: www.moneyformadagascar.org
Lisy Art Gallery, Antanimora, Antananarivo.
Warning: Avoid Antananarivo city centre/Ave de l'Indépendance after dusk – thieving and muggings are rife. Keep passports with you at all times to avoid spot fines.

USEFUL CONTACTS

Embassies have details of medical facilities, including pharmacies, doctors and emergency funds.
American Embassy, tel: 22 43820/43910/43898.
British Embassy, tel: 22 33053. UK Honorary Consul, Mr R. Hyde, tel: 24 5280, ricana@moov.mg http://ukinmadagascar.fco.gov.uk
French Embassy, tel: 22 39898.
German Embassy, tel: 22 223802.
South African Embassy, tel: 22 43350.
GasyCarBus, Antanimena (tel: 26 31754 or 032 53 74507, bus@gasy-car-bus.mg) for bus services to centres such as Toliara, Fianarantsoa and Toamasina.
Madagascar National Parks (formerly ANGAP), contact@madagascar.national.parks.mg www.parcs-madagascar.com
Polyclinique d'Ilafy (Private Hospital): tel: 22 42566/9 or 033 11 458 48 or 032 07 409 38.
Pharmacie Principale, 22 53393, pharm.s@dts.mg
Banks: most have ATMs/cashpoints and some will change travellers cheques though proof of purchase is essential. SOCIMAD provides best rates.

ANTANANARIVO	J	F	M	A	M	J	J	A	S	O	N	D
AVERAGE TEMP. °C	29	29	25	20	17	10	8	8	15	26	29	29
AVERAGE TEMP. °F	84	84	77	68	63	50	46	46	59	79	84	84
RAINFALL mm	270	251	183	51	20	7	11	15	10	67	171	354
RAINFALL in	10.6	9.9	7.2	2	0.8	0.3	0.4	0.6	0.4	2.6	6.7	13.9
DAYS OF RAINFALL	15	14	10	6	3	2	3	4	4	8	12	16

3
Southern Madagascar

With a mostly **semi-arid climate**, white sand **beaches** and a selection of well-run **protected areas**, the south has long been visited by those who want to experience something of the compelling 'uniqueness' of Madagascar. Many visitors arrive in Tuléar after having completed the overland journey along the paved RN7 road from Tana. Others opt for the regular Air Madagascar flights operated between Antananarivo, Fort Dauphin (Tôlañaro) and Tuléar.

The south is known for its **spiny bush** landscape, created by euphorbias and thorny didiera trees interspersed with an array of fascinating bloated and drought-resistant trees and plants. In places, the spiny bush bears a vague resemblance to the Mexican desert at first glance. Anyone exploring the spiny bush would be quick to agree with travel writing legend Dervla Murphy's description of it as 'Nature's botanical lunatic asylum'.

But the southern region is not entirely **semi-desert**: Tôlañaro, on the far southeast coast, marks the limit of the humid eastern domain, and clinging to steep slopes on the high mountains behind the town are the southernmost remnants of montane evergreen forest. Inland, the fascinating three-parcel **national park** of **Andohahela** partly falls into the 'transition zone' between the dry southern and wet eastern domains and also protects one of the southernmost tracts of **rainforest**.

The south coast has long been appreciated for its **marine life**: an extensive barrier reef hugs the southwest coast and, despite bleaching, beckons diving and

Don't Miss

*** **Ifotaka** or **Berenty:** spiny bush, lemurs and Antandroy culture.
*** **Isalo National Park:** mountains, hiking trails and rare wildlife. Combine with Zombitse Forest an hour away.
** **Ifaty spiny bush:** extraordinary flora and rare birds.
** **Lac Tsimanampetsotsa National Park:** scenery seen by few westerners.
** **Anakao:** Veso fishing village, reefs, Nosy Vé beach.

◀ *Opposite: Funerary art of the Antandroy and Mahafaly people (among others) includes wooden carvings which decorate tombs.*

Climate

Because of its predominantly semi-arid climate, the south can be visited year round. Summer days are hot and dry while evenings are pleasant. Winter nights can be very cold. Rainfall is lowest in the southwest (Tuléar region), occurring mainly during February. Fort Dauphin has a pleasant, more humid climate but in September there are forceful winds. It is cooler and less humid than the northeast.

snorkelling enthusiasts. Around Tôlañaro, rock pools delight holiday-makers with their varied and interesting marine life. Madagascar's most visited hiking destination, the **Isalo sandstone massif**, lies about 240km (149 miles) inland from Tuléar. And one of the island's best-known protected areas, **Berenty Private Reserve**, lies 89km (55 miles) inland from Tôlañaro on the Mandrare River bank.

TULÉAR AND SURROUNDS

This seemingly unassuming port is arguably one of the country's most interesting urban centres. The inhabitants include Antandroy, Mahafaly, Masikoro and Veso. In the surrounding countryside – particularly near Andranovory village – some of the most impressive Mahafaly and Antandroy **tombs** may be viewed. To the north and south are the **beach holiday hangouts** of Ifaty and Anakao. Around both locations are tracts of spiny bush.

Tuléar ★

Because of high temperatures and dry heat, most activities in this laid-back town grind to a halt between 11:00 and 15:00. With mudflats instead of beach, Tuléar is generally used as a gateway town to places such as Ifaty, Anakao and Isalo. Currently, the hotels Victory and Hyppocampo provide excellent and comfortable accommodation in Tuléar.

The beach hotel in Anakao routinely collects guests at Tuléar harbour for the speedboat transfers south, generally not later than midday. In Tuléar, the small but endlessly fascinating cultural museum, **Musée Mahafaly-Sakalava** – which displays some extremely rare traditional artefacts, carvings and musical instruments – is a 'must' if you have a cultural interest. Many of the

◀ *Left: The remarkable vegetation of the southern sub-desert is known as the spiny bush. It is dominated by tall, thorny Didiera trees and various other drought-resistant plants and trees, such as at Ifotaka and Ihazo-fotsy in the southeastern interior, and Ifaty, the Mikea Forest and Lac Tsimanam-petsotsa in the southwest.*

items on display are unlikely to be seen elsewhere in the country. As in any of the urban centres, there is a large and colourful **market**, noteworthy for the mohair rugs which are made inland in the area around Ampanihy ('Place of the Bats'). And as with other markets, an enormous variety of ***fanafody*** is sold here. *Fanafody* refers to natural remedies for all sorts of illnesses and conditions, as well as those associated with magic.

Tuléar is one of the urban centres in which getting around is mostly done by means of rickshaw (taxis do not operate after 22:00). Note that while days are generally warm to very hot, winter nights are cool to very cold so pack some warm clothing.

Arboretum de Antsokay ★★★

A delightful botanical garden, Arboretum de Antsokay is about 10 minutes' drive from Tuléar. Established in 1980 by the late botanist and succulent authority Hermann Petignat, this 50ha (123-acre) site showcases the marvellous drought-resistant flora of the spiny bush. It is also home to a wide variety of semi-desert birds, reptiles, the recently described reddish-grey mouse lemur, and all sorts of invertebrates. With the establishment of seed banks for many endangered southern Malagasy plants, the

Southern Tribes and Tombs

Of all the tombs in Madagascar, those belonging to the southern tribes (Mahafaly and Antandroy) are the most spectacular. One of the best roads to see tombs is the RN7 from Tuléar to Isalo. There are several tombs not far from Sakaraha, some of which are topped with *aloalo*. The paintings on the sides of the tombs are worth looking at – there are war and hunting scenes, zebus, mermaids and much more. An interesting contrast is to be seen along the road between Fort Dauphin and Berenty. Now in Antanosy territory, there are memorial sites rather than tombs, with gravestones and obelisks decorated with rows of zebu horns, Christian and pagan symbols. To see more impressive tombs and gain an insight into the intriguing, deep South, adventurous travellers can now go on either small group departures or bespoke individual tours overland across the region.

Arboretum – now run by Mr Petignat's son Andry – continues to make a valuable contribution to the preservation of this fantastic flora (e-mail: andry.petignat@caramail.com). There is a good restaurant, The Dry Forest, and also simple accommodation in the form of bungalows (tel: 032 0260015; www.antsokayarboretum.org).

Ifaty ★★★

Twenty-nine kilometres (18 miles) north of Tuléar along a rough, rutted dirt road, Ifaty has a string of holiday hotels along **sunny beaches**. Offshore, there is a **well-explored reef**. Among other NGOs, the WWF has been active in the Tuléar region for some time, with a view to establishing a marine park and fostering sustainable development. There are **scuba diving** and **water-sports** centres such as those at Les Dunes and Lakana Veso hotels, offering a variety of excursions, with the necessary modern equipment. **Snorkelling** enthusiasts can either arrange boat transport to the reefs – which are some distance offshore – or a pirogue/lakana excursion can be arranged with the help of resident Veso fishermen. (The latter is much more fun and can include a beach barbecue or picnic.) Sadly, however, due to overfishing, the reefs off Ifaty are no longer as rewarding for snorkelling as they once were.

Birders travel here to seek rare southern endemics such as the sub-desert mesite, long-tailed ground-roller and La Fresnaye's vanga. These species inhabit the spiny bush, which in its undisturbed state is dense and tangled. The baobabs you will see are the 'bottle tree' (*Adansonia rubrostipa*), the trunk of which sometimes looks like a gigantic cigar. Blooms of aloes and tall, bloated pachypodiums add welcome splashes of colour to the harsh environment.

The continued destruction of Ifaty's absolutely remarkable spiny bush is alarming. There are three very small, privately protected parcels, all of them degraded to an extent. Birders often go to the smallest, the **Mosa Forest**, where they stand a good chance of ticking off endangered endemics with help from this family of birding guides. Nearby, **Village des Tortues**, run by a French NGO, has a breeding programme for endangered endemic **tortoises** (*see* www.villagetortues.

ReefDoctor in Ifaty

This team of marine biologists has been active around Ifaty since 2002 and concentrates its efforts on the lagoon and barrier reef of Ranobe. The lagoon stretches from the Fiherenana River, past Foret PK32 (where birders and botanists go) up to the Manombo River, just below the fabled Mikea Forest. Toliara's inhabitants are among Madagascar's poorest, and rely largely on the reef for sustenance. With an increase in migrants and with overfishing using destructive techniques, much of Ifaty's marine environment has become degraded. Through a programme of coral reef ecosystem research and monitoring, marine management and community development, ReefDoctor works to inspire the use of sustainable fishing practices among the Veso, as well as developing an understanding of the marine environment and management of its resources for positive development over the short and long term. They work with other NGOs and the Tuléar School Board to implement marine education in local schools. Qualified divers interested in contributing to marine conservation in this fascinating place are invited to participate as volunteers in the ReefDoctor expeditions. *See* www.reefdoctor.org and their blog here: http://reefdoctor.wordpress.com

com). The largest pocket of privately protected spiny bush, Reniala (45ha/111 acres), has many impressive baobabs. Botanists who long to see less-disturbed spiny bush are best off carefully arranging a guided trip further northwards, in the direction of the **Mikea Forest**.

St Augustin Bay ★

Roughly 20km (12 miles) south of Tuléar and almost on the Tropic of Capricorn, St Augustin Bay is one of many former **pirate hide-outs** along the Malagasy coastline. In 1644, British sailor Richard Boothby attempted to establish a settlement. Of the original 120 settlers, only 12 survived and left two years later. The site is now visited primarily by birders, botanists and herpetologists, who also come to La Table hill to seek localized species in the low spiny bush, here known as coral ragg scrub. In place of the bottle baobabs are some impressive greyish moringa trees.

Four kilometres (2.5 miles) down the dirt road from St Augustin is the **Sarodrano Cave**, filled with brackish water. A variety of fish frequent the cave, and some extraordinary reptiles live in the vicinity, including virtually blind snakes and near-limbless skinks.

Currently, due to security issues and lack of reasonable accommodation, St Augustin is visited as a guided day excursion from Tuléar.

Anakao and Nosy Vé ★★

Anakao is a pleasant **Veso village** 56km (35 miles) south of Tuléar. Children play in the sea with their model pirogues, while the men venture far out to sea in the real thing. The sea is safe for **swimming** (but do wear jelly-shoes for the abundant sea urchins) and offshore reefs offer productive **snorkelling** and **diving**. **Surfing** is possible but sharks are common beyond the reef.

Seductive Salary Bay

Turquoise Salary Bay is three hours' drive on a rough dirt road north of Tuléar. Salary Bay Hotel overlooks the exquisite bay. There are 10 rather simple stone bungalows, all with sea view, terrace and hammock, electricity, bathrooms with shower (hot water) and bed with mosquito net. Go swimming, sunbathing, snorkelling, diving, cruising in traditional dhows (*lakana*) and visit the Vezo villages. The hotel has an in-house diving club. Water-skiing, knee-boarding and wake-boarding are offered. Salary can be reached by private charter flight or by speedboat transfer from Tuléar or Ifaty.

▼ *Below: A room at Relais de la Reine d'Isalo, one of Madagascar's finest country hotels.*

▲ *Above: Largest of Madagascar's carnivores is the fosa. At Kirindy, some individuals often visit the camp site.*

In the early 1600s the scrub-covered islet of **Nosy Vé**, 3km (1.8 miles) off Anakao, was a pirate base and the bones of deceased pirates are said to be buried there. It is home to a breeding colony of red-tailed tropicbirds, protected by a strong local *fady* (taboo). Nosy Vé is readily accessible by boat and has a lovely white sand beach, bordered by reefs. On the mainland is the Anakao Ocean Lodge. Guests can organize diving, sailing, kayaking, snorkelling and surfing. They can also arrange a full-day excursion to **Lac Tsimanampetsotsa National Park** by 4WD or quadbikes (based on a minimum of four participants).

Lac Tsimanampetsotsa

Lake Tsimanampetsotsa is a 43,200ha national park 40km (25 miles) inland from Anakao. The lake is a 15km, shallow soda lake surrounded by spiny bush on a limestone plateau. The road from Anakao is rough but the fantastic spiny bush scenery (and limestone caves) amply rewards effort. Look for water birds such as flamingoes (in season), the rare Madagascar plover and lovely Verreaux's coua. There are blind cave gobies, ring-tailed lemurs and highly localized Grandidier's mongoose. Anakao Ocean Lodge offers day excursions to the park (by 4WD in a unimog for a minimum of four people; they will arrange quadbike trips to the lake). Take ample water for the intense dry heat.

Zombitse-Vohibasia National Park ★★★

One hundred and fifty kilometres (93 miles) northeast of Tuléar, straddling the RN7 road to Isalo, **Zombitse Forest** covers roughly 21,500ha (53,000 acres). It is included on all **birding** tour itineraries as one of its residents, the Appert's greenbul, is found nowhere else. Many visitors stopping by at Zombitse also see Madagascar partridge, Madagascar sandgrouse and giant coua. Zombitse is an increasingly rewarding site for spotting fosa in the mating season (early November). It is the only place where ring-tailed lemurs, brown lemurs and Verreaux's sifakas occur together naturally.

At Zombitse the southern and the deciduous western **forest types** meet, creating an odd mix of bamboos, orchids and baobabs (*Adansonia za*); it is also the border of the western and eastern domains, so of high **biological significance**. Getting around the forest which has four easy trails, is not difficult. The reptile fauna is also diverse, with Oustalet's chameleons being particularly abundant. Being accompanied by a professional guide is a requirement. There is now a simple lodge nearby, Zombitse Ecolodge.

Isalo National Park ★★★

The dramatic, if somewhat desolate, landscape created by the Isalo massif's sandstone canyons, cliffs and other formations has become the country's most sought-after **hiking** destination. Existing hotels are often booked up longer in advance than is the case elsewhere in Madagascar. **Isalo National Park** was gazetted in 1962, with 81,540ha (200,000 acres) set aside for protection. Besides its imposing rock formations – referred to as *runiforme* after the French word for 'carved' – flatter areas are covered in grassy vegetation and the tough, low tapia woods. In canyon and valley bottoms are streams bordered by lush greenery and there are some exquisite **natural pools**.

Isalo is situated between Sakaraha, the sapphire town of Iakaka, and Ranohira. There are many sacred and sealed **burial sites** of the Bara people – and some very old Sakalava burial sites – in the rock walls.

Among the circuits is a walk to **Piscine Naturelle** (about 3km/1.8 miles from the vehicle park) and to **Canyon des Makis** (accessible by 4WD or on foot along a rutted track which leads you along a river with a number of pools up to a small waterfall in which you can cool off). The walks are graded as easy to challenging, and the rough, rocky terrain means sturdy footwear is required. Take extra water in your daypack and protection from the strong tropical sun. (That said, autumn and winter nights can be very cold here.)

The Story of Robert Drury

In 1703 the *Degrave* floundered near Fort Dauphin with 160 survivors. Most were killed by the Malagasy but 16-year-old Robert Drury was spared. He spent 17 years as a herd boy and slave, also fighting in intertribal disputes. Yearning for England, Drury crossed the south, built a raft and sailed the Onilahy River to St Augustin. When that village was invaded by the Sakalava, Drury again became a slave until boarding a passing ship to Europe.

▼ *Below: View over the* runiforme *sandstone formations of Isalo National Park.*

Exorcism in Fort Dauphin (Toby)

A centre founded 42 years ago in Fort Dauphin by a woman known as Neni Lava ('old mother') has been filling a gap that might be taken up by psychologists in the West. In Madagascar psychological ailments are often attributed to ancestral demons, and to cure them exorcism rituals have to be performed. Such ceremonies, performed by mediums, can be quite brutal at times, with the 'possessed' bound in chains and beaten, followed by sessions of prayer. 'Patients' may return to Neni Lava's centre as often as they want to, until they feel they have been cured. This treatment has also helped alcoholics and drug addicts. The centre's most important attribute is that it is a venue where people are brought together for holistic healing.

A word of caution: luggage and belongings are not safe if left unguarded in the park. Reputable guides are contactable through a tour operator.

Some of Madagascar's finest country hotels are here: the Colombie family designed and built the splendid Relais de la Reine d'Isalo and its even more luxurious sister hotel, Jardin du Roy. Both have comfortable *en-suite* rooms, a massage centre, sparkling swimming pools and offer horse riding. Top American specialist tour operator Cortez Travel has created the 40-unit Cortez Satrana Lodge, modelled on luxury tented camps in eastern Africa. The latest of the luxury hotels to be built here is Isalo Rock Lodge, fast gaining in popularity.

Wildlife is relatively typical of the semi-arid south, but some fascinating creatures live here. One is the rotund painted burrowing frog, or rainbow frog, with its psychedelic pink, green and pied markings. White-throated rail, Madagascar wagtail and 'Benson's' (forest) rock-thrush inhabit the area, and at night look for Madagascar nightjar and for white-browed owl on the hotel buildings.

Healthy ring-tailed lemurs and Verreaux's sifakas can be seen in the luxuriant vegetation bordering the streams.

Succulents include the so-called 'elephant's foot' pachypodium, a squat, bloated plant that grows on the

sandstone cliffs and blooms in September. Some rare palms are local to the massif.

Permits can be arranged through your tour operator to save yourself the hassle.

Tuléar to Fort Dauphin/Tôlañaro

The distance from Tuléar to Fort Dauphin/Tôlañaro is roughly 650km (400 miles), which should be made in at least five days to really get a feel for this part of the country. Organized carefully, and with the help of the right people, it can be a marvellous **adventure trip** for those who are tolerant of basic conditions.

Currently the road is rough (very rough, rutted and/or rocky in places), so 4WD vehicles are used. Along the journey you can become acquainted with the culture of the Mahafaly, Antandroy and Antanosy people. The Androy is a harsh but fascinating land of spiny bush, baobabs, colourful tombs, amazing funerary art, mohair carpet weavers, zebu ox carts, markets, remote villages and so much more.

◀ Opposite: The streams in Isalo's canyons feature green belts of vegetation including rare palms. There are lovely natural pools and camp sites in the canyons.

▼ Below: Best known of Madagascar's many endemic pachypodiums is the 'elephant's foot', which clings to rock faces in Isalo and blooms in September.

FORT DAUPHIN (TÔLAÑARO) AND SURROUNDS

Fort Dauphin (or Tôlañaro) was the site of the **first European settlement** in Madagascar. Shipwrecked Portuguese sailors built the old fort near the **Ambinanibe River** in 1504, but by 1527 they were driven into the nearby mountains by Antanosy. There they either succumbed to disease or were killed. In 1642, a Frenchman, Sieur Pronis, arrived with an expedition at scenic Baie de Sainte-Luce to establish a trading post and a foothold for the French. Pronis and friends subsequently left Ste-Luce for a site further south, where they constructed Fort Flacourt and named

the settlement Fort Dauphin, after the then child prince, Dauphin, who would later assume the title **Louis XIV**. The Pronis settlement failed exactly as the earlier Portuguese attempt had and was abandoned in 1674.

Pirates and **slave traders** operating in the early 1700s suffered some dismal experiences in this part of Madagascar: there were instances where shipwrecked sailors and other nefarious characters would arrive, only for the Antanosy to take them in and use them as slaves instead.

Fort Dauphin/Tôlañaro ★

This attractively situated town has been modernized considerably during the last few years. Primarily as a result of the Rio Tinto/QMM mining activities, international transport links have been established and the port has been redeveloped. The peninsula on which Tôlañaro is set is flanked by sweeping, sandy **beaches** off which **surfing** is good. To the north are high mountains, with **Pic St Louis** overlooking the town. To cater for the influx of visitors and residents, new hotels of an international standard, such as the Sunny and Colbert, have opened. While **Berenty Private Reserve** remains the island's best-known wildlife hot spot and Tôlañaro's single biggest tourist attraction, some marvellous new options are now available, catering for the most discerning of travellers.

Energetic visitors who would like to enjoy a breathtaking view over Fort Dauphin can make a day trip to the 529m (1735ft) Pic St Louis. The ascent takes roughly two hours and being accompanied by a local guide in this area is

◀ *Left: The southeastern corner of Madagascar has some beautiful bays, such as Lokaro and Baie de Sainte-Luce.*

essential, for security reasons. (There has been a spate of muggings and sexual assaults in the Tôlañaro area during the last few years.)

Baie de Sainte-Luce, Evatra and Lokaro ★★

Sixty-three kilometres (39 miles) from Tôlañaro, at tranquil Baie de Sainte-Luce (Manafiafy), the De Heaulme family (who own Berenty and its associated hotels in Tôlañaro) have a small private reserve which protects a patch of east coast littoral forest.

The Lokaro peninsula, about 10km (6 miles) from Fort Dauphin, contains a system of waterways, lakes and canals in verdant countryside. Visitors enjoy guided **pirogue trips** along the waterways, ending at the Antanosy village of Evatra. This can be arranged by Air Fort Services. Lokaro Bay – an hour's walk from Evatra – has beautiful sand beaches and massive waves. The countryside is worth exploring for its orchids, reptiles and frogs.

Edward Tucker-Brown and his team, who own Mandrare River Camp, opened a superb lodge in this area, Manafiafy Beach & Rainforest Lodge, which in combination with Mandrare River Camp makes for a wonderful holiday.

Mandena Conservation Site

This 230ha (568-acre) patch of southeast coastal littoral forest and wetland was recently established by the Rio Tinto/QMM to protect the most intact portion of forest in the area where mining operations are taking place. Mandena has been sensitively planned with the local Antanosy community involved in running the park. There is an enjoyable two- to three-hour circuit through the verdant surrounds and much small wildlife to be seen. Lemurs include a troop of the the rare collared brown lemur. The site is a lovely 10km (6 miles) drive from Tôlañaro. Day excursions can be arranged through your hotel or tour operator. Note that boat transfers to the site can be harrowing because of rough seas.

Nahampoahana Wildlife Sanctuary

Just 15 minutes' drive from Tôlañaro, this 65ha (160-acre) **arboretum/nature reserve** owned by Air Fort Services protects flourishing populations of various **lemur** species, along with other smaller wildlife in picturesque surrounds, including a canal and waterfall. Wildlife tour groups love the place, as photographic opportunities are outstanding.

Malagasy Guides

In almost all Madagascar's protected areas it is compulsory to hire a local guide. Most are excellent, intimately familiar with the terrain, and without their skills, visitors would miss much of what the sites have to offer. Guides can be contacted either at the sites of interest, through your tour operator, or through nearby hotels. Prospective visitors need to be aware that while the services of a local guide may be confirmed long in advance, their services cannot be guaranteed, due to unforeseen factors such as malaria. Check the Madagascar National Park website for the latest information on guiding fees and permits as these do vary across the country. If you are happy with your guide's services, by all means give a tip or gift. When doing so, please take into consideration that many guides earn more than junior doctors do.

BERENTY PRIVATE RESERVE

On the bank of the wide, shallow Mandrare River, Berenty is 89km (55 miles) west of Fort Dauphin along a dreadful road. Set in a sea of **sisal plantations**, Berenty protects dry tamarind gallery woodland and a small patch of spiny bush. To visit here you must stay at a De Heaulme-owned hotel should your itinerary include a night in Fort Dauphin. They will arrange transportation to the reserve, but will not collect you from – or take you back to – other hotels. (Pack an inflatable neck-pillow to cushion your spine during the road transfers). The best of the De Heaulme-owned hotels is currently the **Croix du Sud**, with its *en-suite* rooms built around a courtyard.

Note that although the Gîte d'Berenty Lodge has *en-suite* bungalows and recently (2007) underwent some maintenance, it is simple and adequate and still in need of some refurbishment. Electricity is not supplied 24/7, so if you enjoy bedtime reading, take a halogen lamp. The restaurant has a limited menu, so you may wish to take some snacks along. But keep any food secure in your baggage, as cheeky ring-tailed lemurs quickly raid the 14 rooms and 14 bungalows.

There is a useful information centre and an excellent small **cultural** and **natural history museum**. The museum has examples of erotic Sakalava carvings that are now nearly impossible to see in the Menabe where they originate from. There are also artefacts of the Antandroy who live here.

Getting to Berenty

From Tôlañaro a variable road heads west towards the **Anosyenne mountains**, where the last of the southernmost rainforests cling to steep slopes. After crossing the fascinating 'transition zone' between the eastern and southern domains (where you can stop to see the endangered **triangle palm**), the spiny bush stretches out for as far as the eye can see. Although there appear to be large areas of this seemingly impenetrable bush left, it is disappearing fast. The main reason is charcoal production to satisfy demand for fuel in Tôlañaro. The baobabs you will pass by are of the large southern species *Adansonia za*.

Amboasary, the last sizeable town before Berenty, was a base for the SOS Sud Food Aid Programme carried out during the prolonged drought which struck here in the 1980s and early 1990s. The interesting villages along the road, with their tiny square huts built out of wood, are those of the Antandroy, the 'People of the Thorns'. Villages are often surrounded by fences constructed either of *raketa* (prickly pear) cactus or alluaudia trees.

Berenty Private Reserve ★★

To a large extent Berenty was put on the map by leading lemur expert Lady Alison Jolly, who has conducted research

Coton de Tuléar

The Coton de Tuléar is Madagascar's 'official' dog. Its ancestors were possibly brought to Madagascar in the 16th century by sailors from Spain and Portugal. The Coton – which looks something like a Maltese poodle – is thought to be part of the Bichon dog family, perhaps linked most closely to the extinct Bichon Tenerife. The latter was introduced to nearby Mauritius and Réunion by sailors in the 16th–17th centuries. The breed then acquired its cottony coat which is thought to be due to a single gene mutation. Known then as the Coton de Réunion, they became the companions of pirates, merchants and noblemen travellers. These small, friendly dogs were treasured by Merina monarchs, and were bred into the existing Coton de Tuléar dogs, which are widely kept in Europe and North America.

◀◀ Opposite: Madagascar tree boa, one of three species of boa unique to the island. The family also exists in South America but not Africa.
◀ Left: Two species of pitcher plant are found in Madagascar, the westernmost limit of these carnivorous plants.

Responsible Travel: Litter

Keep all litter in your possession until you find suitable disposal facilities. Dispose of cigarettes and matches with care: much of Madagascar is dry for most of the year and fires can devastate the fragile ecosystems.

here for 40 years. Lady Jolly still returns annually and her written work – which includes the delightful book *Lords and Lemurs* – popularized Berenty and drew attention to Madagascar's environmental crisis.

Berenty is one of few reserves in which visitors may wander about **unguided**, as the network of broad and well-maintained paths is simple and the reserve is small (258ha/637 acres). Early mornings are most rewarding for wildlife viewing in any Malagasy forest, so it is advisable to stay for at least one night. This means you can also take in a night walk.

Most people come to Berenty for a good 'fix' of lemurs, and they do not leave disappointed. The iconic ring-tails are very tame, allowing for brilliant **photo opportunities**. The 'dancing' Verreaux's sifakas are the other firm favourite, particularly when they descend to the ground and hop around like participants in a sack race. Unfortunately some of the ring-tails living around the lodge seasonally lose patches of their fur as a result of feeding on a toxic introduced plant, leucaena. This is currently being eradicated by management and the lemurs' fur re-grows in the summer months. The brown lemurs present here are hybrids between red-fronted brown and collared brown lemurs.

Nocturnal wildlife includes the white-footed sportive lemur, grey mouse lemur and the common tenrec. There is a large, raucous colony of '**flying foxes**' (Madagascar fruit bats). Reptiles include the Malagasy ground boa and the warty and jewel chameleons. Bird-wise, Berenty is possibly the best stakeout for white-browed owl, Madagascar cuckoo-hawk and the stately giant coua with its blue face mask. It is an excellent site for the delightful hissing cockroach, large groups of which can be seen in certain trees at night.

▶ *Opposite: The endearing Verreaux's sifaka is easily seen in Berenty, where a large and well-habituated population exists. It can also be seen in Isalo, Zombitse, Ifotaka, Ihazofotsy and in Kirindy.*
▼ *Below: Travel writing legend Dervla Murphy aptly labelled the southern spiny bush as 'Nature's botanical lunatic asylum'.*

ANDOHAHELA NATIONAL PARK

Split into three parcels – **Malio** (rainforest), **Tsimelahy** (transition forest) and **Ihazofotsy** (spiny bush) – this magnificent park encapsulates a wider spectrum of forest types than any other in the country. The park opened in 1998 and presently facilities are limited. It is possible to visit Tsimelahy and Ihazofotsy as a full-day excursion provided you travel in a **4WD vehicle** with a professional guide.

Tsimelahy is only about 90 minutes inland from Tôlañaro, some 8km (5 miles) north of the road from Amboasary. Aside from protecting a substantial population of the highly localized and endangered **triangle palm**, there are baobabs, tall pachypodiums, alluaudia trees and a wealth of small wildlife in beautiful surrounds.

Ihazofotsy protects **spiny bush** which is in good condition. The parcel is sparsely inhabited, and the lemur species protected here include ring-tails and Verreaux's sifakas. Ihazofotsy also offers rewarding birding and has a rich reptile fauna.

Malio, the rainforest parcel, is mostly known to **birders**, **herpetologists**, **entomologists** and **botanists**. The rare collared lemur is present, as is the southern lesser bamboo lemur, but they are not well habituated so sightings cannot be guaranteed. Birders come to look for the

Responsible Travel: Conservation and Pollution

Try to use environmentally friendly toiletries and to do so sparingly to minimize the pollution of local water supplies. Switch off lights, fans and air conditioners when leaving your room.

Don't squander water. Be aware there are water shortages in parts of the country, notably the south. If there are shortages, try to be sensitive about how much personal water you use because it can have wide-ranging effects on local agriculture and livelihoods.

Avoid souvenirs that endanger any species, including tortoiseshell, seashells and any other wildlife products. It is strictly forbidden to remove indigenous plants or their seeds from Madagascar and the penalties are severe.

Try to purchase locally produced, rather than imported, goods and visit small-scale souvenir shops. Keep your receipts for objects made of wood.

Visiting and supporting local conservation and community projects provides valuable funds for these initiatives. The consequent improvement in living standards is an important source of encouragement to local communities.

▲ *Above: The ring-tailed lemur – Madagascar's national animal.*

enigmatic red-tailed newtonia. Malio can be visited as a day trip from Tôlañaro.

IFOTAKA COMMUNITY FOREST

Ifotaka is a community-managed forest a 45-minute drive further inland than Berenty is from Fort Dauphin. The Antandroy communities here preserve parts of the forest for **ecotourism** and also parts which are sacred (*ala fady*). Elsewhere, cattle grazing and wood cutting is permitted. The habitat holds much the same wildlife as are present in Berenty. Fees generated from tourism go directly to the local communities.

Madagascar Classic Camping in Ifotaka

From April to October, when weather conditions are pleasant, discerning travellers can explore spiny bush and gallery woods in style, thanks to Madagascar's first luxury **tented camp**. Each of Madagascar Classic Camping's six large (17m^2) tents has a comfortable, netted, four-poster bed, high-quality wooden furniture, electric lighting and private *en-suite* facilities, including a biodegradable chemi-loo, safari shower and BioAroma toiletries. Each also has a furnished verandah. Electricity is provided by means of environmentally friendly solar panels.

Sumptuous and elegantly presented meals are served in the main tent. Guests are able to learn about the fascinating traditions of the Antandroy people; you will be able to see **tombs**, enjoy **performances** by Antandroy dancers and musicians, visit a **market**, and if there is one happening during your visit, you may even attend a ***ringa*** (wrestling) contest.

It appears that access is now permitted to a sacred forest where sightings of habituated ringtail lemurs are virtually guaranteed.

Best Times to Visit

Much of the region is arid so can be visited **all year**. In the brief rainy season (January–March) it is extremely hot. In autumn and winter (May–August) days are mild to warm and nights can be very cold.

Getting There

The most popular and most worthwhile overland trip on Madagascar is the **Route National 7** (RN7) road from Tana southwest to Tuléar. It is ideally completed in about 10–14 days, and is now fully paved. **Air Madagascar** operates several flights a week from Tana to Tuléar and to Fort Dauphin. Flight schedules are changed twice yearly and sometimes in between.

Getting Around

There are **flights** connecting Tuléar to Fort Dauphin and to Morondava. The road from Ihosy to Fort Dauphin is in poor condition (2013) but if taken on by 4WD over a few days with an experienced guide, and if arranged through a reputable operator such as Asisten-Travel (info@asisten-travel.com www.asisten-travel.com) it can be a truly fascinating adventure for those who do not mind roughing it. Most visitors use Tuléar and Fort Dauphin only as gateway towns to attractions profiled in this book. **Rickshaws** are a popular means of transport in Tuléar, especially later at night when taxis do not operate. It's a fun way to get to/from the infamous Club Za-za, where people party into the early hours to stomping but kitsch, crossover club music. Tuléar has a good crafts market. Refrain from purchasing sea shells, because some of the species sold here are now critically endangered. Anakao is best reached by speedboat transfers from Tuléar harbour. The road to Ifaty is in poor, deeply rutted condition. The road from Fort Dauphin to Berenty Private Reserve has deteriorated and the drive there, with stops, now takes about four hours. In Fort Dauphin and Tuléar, **taxis** are cheap and readily available.

Where to Stay

Tuléar

Luxury

Hyppocampo, tel: 20 94 4102, info@hyppocampo.com www.hyppocampo-tulear.com The hotel of choice in Tuléar. A courtyard garden surrounds the pool; sea view bar, sheltered terrace and massage room. Eight double rooms and two suites overlook the garden and have sea views. The only drawback is the caged lemurs.

Mid-range

Hotel Victory, tel: 94 44060. Seventeen spacious rooms with aircon, TV and phone, relaxed ambience, swimming pool. Indian and Malagasy cuisine. In a quiet area on Route de l'Aerport.

Budget

Chez Alain, tel: 94 41527, c.alain@moov.net www.chez-alain.net Twenty-one rooms in a lovely garden. One of Tuléar's best-known hotels for its excellent restaurant. They hire mountain bicycles.

Ifaty Beach

Luxury

Hotel Les Dunes, BP 285, Tuléar, tel: 22 25812, dunesifaty@apma.mg www.lesdunesdifaty.com Recently refurbished with 22 rooms and 19 bungalows, and now the best hotel in Ifaty. It has a very good restaurant. Highly praised.

Le Paradisier, tel: 94 42914, paradisier@paradisier.net www.paradisier.net Comfortable bungalows, swimming pool, good service and excellent food. Book in advance.

La Mira, tel: 032 0262144. Small hotel to the north of Ifaty, with nine airy, *en-suite* rooms. Excellent food and highly praised for its service. Best choice for visiting birders.

Mid-range

Vovo Telo, tel: 94 93718, hotelvovotelo@simicro.mg www.hotel-vovotelo.com Popular small hotel with 16 bungalows. Only down side is the noisy nightclub.

Salary Bay, tel: 075 51486, salarybay@malagasy.com www.salarybay.com Ten comfortable *en-suite* bungalows, in a beautiful beach location. They offer snorkelling, scuba diving and boat excursions, as well as walks in the fascinating Mikea Forest. Salary is a Veso village at a beautiful beach, accessible by speedboat from Ifaty.

Anakao

Luxury

Anakao Ocean Lodge, tel: 094 91957, eres@lifehospitality.com www.anakao-madagascar.com tel: 20 94 91957/92176, anakaooceanlodge@gmail.com This is the best hotel in Anakao. Activities available here include scuba diving, snorkelling at Nosy Vé, fishing and kayaking, and they can also arrange trips to Lac Tsimanampetsotsa. The lodge is beautifully designed, with excellent service and good food; extras are expensive.

Mid-range

Zombitse-Vohibasia Forest National Park, Zombitse Ecolodge tel: 033 1232564, www.zombitse.de At last, there is now some permanent albeit basic accommodation servicing this exceptional wildlife hotspot: 10 basic bungalows (3 *en suite*), 7km from the park entrance and 10km east of Sakaraha. A professional guide can arrange permits and local guides for the four circuits. (Visitors should be accompanied by a guide and driver from Antananarivo.)

Isalo

Luxury

Jardin du Roy, three blocks of luxurious *en-suite* rooms, a big swimming pool and superb food and service make this the best hotel in the area. Owned and designed by the Colombier family who also own Le Relais la Reine d'Isalo (*see* below).

Le Relais la Reine d'Isalo, BP 1, Ranohira, tel: 022 33623 (c/o Madagascar Discovery Agency), www.hotels-isalo.com Solid, spacious chalets beautifully designed to blend into the massif. Swimming pool; horse riding can be arranged. Top-notch cuisine and service. Book well in advance.

Cortez Satrana, tel: 261 2022 219-74, www.hotel-isalo-lodge.com Luxury tented camp owned by USA's leading Madagascar specialist, Cortez Travel. Book through their Antananarivo branch (Cortez Expeditions: 25 rue Ny Zafindriandiky, Antanimena).

Isalo Rock Lodge, tel/fax: 20 22 32860, gm@isalorocklodge.com or reservations@isalorocklodge.com www.isalorocklodge.com Sixty comfortable *en-suite* rooms with stunning views; the lodge is well located in the massif and a favourite with discerning clients visiting Isalo. Rooms are air conditioned and there is a swimming pool. Please note there are occasional power outages here.

Mid-range

Isalo Ranch, tel: 22 30928, www.isalo-ranch.com Popular hotel, recently refurbished with 19 bungalows and a sparkling swimming pool; transport can be arranged to/from Isalo National Park. Book well in advance.

Fort Dauphin (Tôlañaro)

Mid-range

Kaleta Hotel, tel: 20 92 21287, kaletaresa@moov.mg Has 40 air-conditioned rooms with a big suite, 5 senior and 5 junior suites and 29 standard rooms, safety box, mini bar, satellite TV. Well located and preferred by business-people. Currently the best property in town.

Mid-range

Croix du Sud, Safari Tours du Capricorne, BP 54, Fort Dauphin, tel: 92 21238. Owned by the De Heaulme family, who own Berenty. 32 simple *en-suite* rooms neatly built around a central courtyard. Can cater for tour groups. If visiting Berenty with an overnight stay in Fort Dauphin, you are required to stay here. Meals taken in its basic sister hotel Le Dauphin.

Lavasoa, tel: 3312 51703, info@lavasoa.mg www.lavasoa.com Lovely little hotel with just five *en-suite* bungalows; excellent and attentive service. Breakfasts are served, but not other meals. Best location in town, overlooking the picturesque

Libanona Beach. They offer 4WD trips to local sites of interest, including trips to Lokaro Bay.

Berenty
MID-RANGE
Gîte d'Berenty Lodge, tel: 92 21238. Fourteen simple, *en-suite* bungalows and 14 simple rooms; restaurant with limited menu; interesting museum. Book through Hotel Le Dauphin or Croix du Sud. Electricity is not supplied 24/7 at this lodge. Book long in advance. Being accompanied by an English-speaking guide is advised.

Ifotaka
Mandrare River Camp, tel/fax: 22 02226 or 032 0561900, information@madaclassic.com or Erika@madaclassic.com www.madaclassic.com This is Madagascar's first luxury tented camp. Impeccable service; a highly recommended site at Ifotaka. Book long in advance to avoid disappointment.
Manafiafy Rainforest and Beach Lodge, tel: 032 5161900. Recently opened by Tucker-Brown (proprietor of Mandrare River Camp), in a beautiful, secluded bay at Baie St Luce. Fronted by a white sand beach and amid east coast littoral forest, the 4 luxury bungalows and 2 family villas offer top notch accommodation with *en-suite* facilities, hot water and are totally solar powered. Spending three or more nights here makes for a perfect combination with Mandrare River Camp. Whale watching in the area can be spectacular from June to September. Forest walks and boat trips are offered and snorkelling is good (there is also safe swimming).

Where to Eat

Tuléar
Restaurante Etoile de Mer, tel: 094 42807, on the seafront, serves Indian, Afghan and Italian dishes and wonderful seafood.
Le Panda offers good Chinese meals.
Chez Alain's restaurant is a long-established favourite.

Fort Dauphin (Tôlañaro)
The island is lobster capital; the listed hotels all serve excellent meals.
The simple **Mahavoky Annexe** is an old favorite and has a convivial vibe.
Las Vegas, tel: 032 11 53055. This restaurant serves Malagasy and Italian dishes; relaxed terrace.

Shopping

Tuléar, a centre of the Mahafaly, Antandroy and Veso people, has an interesting market where some wonderful mohair rugs, colourful *lambas*, and sometimes southwestern tribal artefacts – including masks – may be found.

Tours and Excursions

Fort Dauphin (Tôlañaro)
Air Fort Services, BP 159, Fort Dauphin, tel: 92 212 24/34, air.fort@wanadoo.mg www.airfortservices.com Car and light aircraft rental; various excursions; guides and provisions for trekking. Shopping trips to local villages. Owners of Nahampoahana Wildlife Sanctuary.

Tuléar
Regional Tourist Office, Boulevard Gallieni, tel: 094 44605 or 032 0760677, ortu@tulear-tourisme.com www.tulear-tourisme.com

Useful Contacts

Tuléar
Clinique Saint Luc (medical clinic), tel: 94 42247.
Centre Hopital Regional, tel: 94 41855. Scuba divers should note that this hospital is equipped to handle diving-related problems.

TULÉAR	J	F	M	A	M	J	J	A	S	O	N	D
AVERAGE TEMP. °C	33	32	32	30	30	27	26	25	29	30	32	32
AVERAGE TEMP. °F	91	90	90	86	86	81	79	77	84	86	90	90
RAINFALL mm	94	89	36	18	16	15	6	6	8	12	22	97
RAINFALL in	3.7	3.5	1.4	0.7	0.6	0.6	0.2	0.2	0.3	0.5	0.9	3.8
DAYS OF RAINFALL	6	5	3	2	2	2	1	1	2	2	3	4

4. Western Madagascar

Some of the country's **hallmark images** originate from the western region: the ***tsingy*** plateaus with their limestone pinnacle-fields and the impressive baobab forests are just two. The western, seasonally dry deciduous forests are Madagascar's most threatened and fragmented forest type with less than 2% remaining. Consequently, the threatened animals living in these frail, slow-growing forests are a high conservation priority. Secluded white sand beaches in discrete locations such as Anjajavy are a perfect choice for **relaxing getaways**. The west is Sakalava country, with the Menabe sub-tribe centred around Morondava and the Boina around the port of Mahajanga.

The great Sakalava kingdom originated in the 1600s, and later split broadly into the Menabe and Boina. These people portray noticeably African characteristics, the result of influxes of settlers from East Africa. Possibly best known of the many clans are the Veso, who reside along the coast. They are expert fishermen, sailors and boat builders.

Don't Miss

★★★ **Ankarafantsika National Park:** wildlife hot spot extraordinaire!
★★★ **Anjajavy:** Madagascar's best accommodation, sunny beaches and baobab forests.
★★ **Tsingy de Bemaraha National Park:** otherworldly scenery and the Manambolo River nearby.
★★ **Kirindy Forest** and **Alley of Giant Baobabs**.

◀ *Opposite: One of Madagascar's hallmark images is the Alley of Giant Baobabs just north of Morondava.*

MAHAJANGA

Mahajanga ★

The 'place of the red rocks', Mahajanga is Madagascar's second-largest port and lies at the mouth of one of the country's biggest rivers, the **Betsiboka**. The river is often referred to as one of the island's 'incurable bleeding arteries', i.e. rivers which, as the result of extensive erosion inland, stain the sea a brownish-red colour.

Mahajanga is a **lively** place, and with plenty of taxis, buses and rickshaws it is easy to get around. The sprawl-

ing market is usually good for **souvenirs** such as *lambas* and colourful beads, or *vakana*. This is the main mango-producing region and much of the crop is dried and exported. Prawns are also farmed. Local baobabs are of the fatter, African variety, and include a gigantic specimen in the town centre.

Mahajanga can be reached either by regular Air Madagascar flights from Tana or Nosy Bé, or by road on the RN4. The latter option takes eight hours and until Ankarafantsika National Park, there isn't much to see.

Ankarafantsika National Park ('Ampijoroa') ★★★

Lying 130km (80 miles) inland from Mahajanga, a two-hour trip along a good tarmac road, this is a magnificent example of western seasonally dry forest. So rewarding is **wildlife** viewing here, that the 130,000ha (321,230-acre) Ankarafantsika is included in most natural history itineraries. Because the canopy of deciduous woodlands is lower and more open than that of the eastern rainforests, viewing wildlife is generally easier.

There is a conveniently designed network of **paths**, some of which begin at the 'Ampijoroa' camp site. They are graded 'easy', are on gentle terrain, and most take a few hours to complete. The Gîte d'Ampijoroa has some comfortable *en-suite* **bungalows** across the road by Lac Ravelobe. The gîte also has a block of small rooms at the **camp site**, with electricity and shared ablution facilities (funded by the KFW), as well as a small, open-air **restaurant** called La Pigargue.

Wildlife at Ankarafantsika ***

One of the highlights of a visit to Ankarafantsika is the **Durrell Wildlife Conservation Trust**'s largest Madagascar-based project, '**Project Angonoka**', based adjacent to the camp site. Thanks to the dedicated efforts of the DWCT, the ploughshare tortoise (*angonoka*), the rarest land tortoise in the world, has been saved from extinction. At the site, the DWCT are also breeding the peculiar little flat-tailed tortoise or *kapidolo,* which refers to the species often being found in small, sacred patches of forest around tombs (*lolo*) in the Menabe.

Acrobatic Coquerel's sifakas live around the camp site so they are easily seen. Most visitors also see the common brown lemur with its characteristic black face, and the local guides generally find dozy Milne-Edward's sportive lemurs in their tree holes, as well as the larger western woolly lemur in matted vegetation. Grey and golden-brown mouse lemurs can be seen at night. The rare and crepuscular mongoose lemur, which is best sought in Ampijoroa, is identifiable by its white snout.

Climate

The western lowlands have summer rains, most of which fall from January to March. **Winter** days are **warm** and evenings always pleasant while **summer** days are **very hot**, temperatures averaging around the 40°C (104°F) mark. Around Mahajanga there are often cool breezes, but not so in Morondava or the forests near both these towns, where it can be baking hot from about 08:00.

▼ *Below: The paths in Ankarafantsika National Park ('Ampijoroa') are broad and well maintained. It is arguably the most rewarding wildlife hot spot in western Madagascar and ANGAP has established comfortable accommodation.*

FANAMBY

One of the most proactive and successful Malagasy NGOs, FANAMBY was founded in 1997 by Serge Rajaobelina, and their projects emphasize local community development and development of responsible tourism in some fascinating places. These include Kirindy Forest, which received formal protection only in 2006. They also work in the highly fragmented forest site of Daraina (which holds, among other lemurs, the critically endangered golden-crowned sifaka), and at Anjorobe. *See* www.fanamby.wordpress.com

Common reptiles are the giant hog-nosed snake and the rhinoceros chameleon, as well as the collared iguanid lizard, whose nearest relatives are in South America. Leaf-tailed geckoes present are the bark-mimicking Henkel's leaf-tailed gecko and the rarely seen Guenther's leaf-tailed gecko. Greener-than-green day geckoes add startling splashes of colour to tree trunks.

Ankarafantsika appears on all **birding** itineraries as it is the only accessible site where all the western forest-dependent endemics can be ticked off. Birders come from around the globe to seek the comical white-breasted mesite, Coquerel's coua, the lovely Schlegel's asity and the localized Van Dam's vanga. There is also a pair of the critically endangered Madagascar fish eagles resident around **Lac Ravelobe**. (Please note that this lake is not suitable for swimming in; crocodiles have attacked a number of people in the last decade and there is a resistant strain of giardia.)

Book the gîte long in advance, especially if you are travelling in the austral spring (September to November). Reservations are best made through a tour operator.

▼ *Below: A male ploughshare tortoise in the breeding centre at Ankarafantsika National Park ('Ampijoroa'), where it has been saved from extinction.*

Katsepy ★

Across the **Betsiboka Delta** from Mahajanga harbour, this village is accessible by daily ferry. The woods near the lighthouse, and the forest of Antrema, hold the critically endangered **crowned sifaka** and some mongoose lemurs. Chez Chabaud in Katsepy offers comfortable, spacious *en-suite* bungalows, and here is one of the two restaurants (the other is in Mahajanga) run by the Chabaud sisters, Brigitte and Christiane. Both restaurants have had a loyal, international following for many years. The sisters, who took over from their late mother, the legendary **Madame Chabaud**, are excellent hosts,

◀ *Left: The critically endangered Coquerel's sifaka is easily seen at Ankarafantsika and at Anjajavy, where groups of these endearing lemurs have become very confiding.*

and the food is always a treat. *See* http://chabaudlodge.wifeo.com or contact tel: 20 62 23327.

Cirque Rouge and Antsanitia ★

A short drive from Mahajanga, Cirque Rouge is an eroded **canyon** with various red-clay formations that look best at sunset or just before a storm. Nearby Amborovy has a safe **swimming** beach. An hour's drive from Mahajanga by rough road, the stylish Antsanitia Resort has a lovely beach and makes for an enjoyable place to unwind after visiting Ankarafantsika.

ANJAJAVY

Madagascar's sole Relais & Chateaux property, Anjajavy is on a remote, forested peninsula and, uniquely, it combines luxury accommodation, superb food and the excellent hospitality of a beach resort with captivating scenery and a 450ha (1112-acre) tropical deciduous forest reserve.

Two prominent features in the area are an abundance of **baobabs** (mostly the large *Adansonia madagascariensis*) in all shapes and forms, and **limestone formations** on the forest floor. The beach is lovely and offers safe swimming.

There are 24 glass-fronted, air-conditioned rosewood villas, each with a furnished verandah on which visitors can luxuriate in a hammock. A variety of **water sports** is on offer; the deep-sea fishing is exceptional. During guided walk along one of the **trails** into the forest you should

Tromba

The core of Sakalava spirituality, *tromba* refers to spirits, or possession by spirits, usually royal or common ancestors. Royalty are the most influential *tromba* as they belong to all. The *tromba* experience occurs during any significant social event. *Tromba* spirits have also manifested in members of congregations at Christian church services. Most mediums are women and most *tromba* spirits are masculine. Most observers are women, and the spirit interpreters are men. Possession is often preceded by acute symptoms such as headaches, body pains and stomach ache. The possessed seek help from doctors, herbalists and mediums, inevitably to be told their symptoms are due to resistance to *tromba*. If a medium confirms diagnosis as *tromba*, the possessed must undergo various ceremonies/rites. The *tromba* spirit will then inhabit the new medium occasionally, otherwise remaining in the tomb. During possession, the medium's own spirit is temporarily displaced so she doesn't remember anything, hence the use of interpreters. A medium may have multiple spirits possessing her at different times.

▲ *Above: Aerial view of the exclusive Anjajavy L'Hotel, fronted by a white sand beach and surrounded by wildlife-rich seasonally dry forest.*

encounter a troop or two of Coquerel's sifaka, which also enter the lush gardens daily. There are brown lemurs and, at night, an abundance of mouse lemurs and noisy sportive lemurs. Reptiles include the gigantic Oustalet's chameleon, collared iguanid lizard and the giant hog-nose snake. In late spring and summer (from late November) visitors may see a few species of frog during night strolls.

The area is known for its rich **bird life**: at least two pairs of the last remaining 200-odd Madagascar fish eagles have territories here and are easily spotted. In the mangroves, endangered Madagascar white ibis are seen. Crested and Coquerel's couas, Madagascar lesser cuckoo, noisy greater vasa parrots and Madagascar hoopoe are all common in the reserve. A boat trip to **Moramba Bay** takes you to small islets eroded into mushroom-like shapes. Some of these have caves, and certain caves are Sakalava **burial sites**. Because it is *fady* for pigs to walk over a Sakalava grave, influential members of the community have their burial sites in such virtually inaccessible caves.

In the hotel gardens, particularly at the beautifully landscaped **L'Oasis** where tea is served in the afternoons, you can see flocks of grey-headed lovebirds, bright red Madagascar fodys and gangs of garrulous sickle-billed vangas. Sakalava weavers suspend their kidney-shaped nests below the eaves of the main hotel building.

Giant Jumping Rat

One of Kirindy's most unusual denizens is the endearing and endangered giant jumping rat. Called the *vozitse* by the Malagasy, it is the biggest Malagasy rodent, the same size as a hare. It has a bulbous pink nose, a honey-coloured body and strong back legs on which it can bound, kangaroo-style. The Durrell Wildlife Conservation Trust took a few specimens to the Jersey Zoo on loan from the Malagasy government and captive breeding has been very successful. It is best sought just after the first rains begin.

Anjajavy's management funds a tree nursery where endangered endemic hardwoods are cultivated to ensure the future of the forest. They also support a market garden to reduce 'food miles' and are the sole employer in this remote site, accessible only by light aircraft. Flights are operated three times a week from Tana to Anjajavy. The required minimum stay is three nights.

MORONDAVA AND SURROUNDS

If any Malagasy town resembles something from a Wild West movie set, this is it. The gateway town to **Kirindy Forest** is famed for its numerous baobabs, particularly the massive Grandidier's baobab, largest of its family. The 60km (37-mile) drive to Kirindy takes you through a national monument and World Heritage Site, the **Alley of Giant Baobabs**.

Until recent years, slash-and-burn and illegal logging were problematic here, but have recently been taken under control – at least until 2009. Two NGOs hard at work to conserve this forest with the participation of local communities are the **DWCT** and **FANAMBY**. Morondava is one of the hottest places in the country, with temperatures around the 40°C (104°F) mark not being uncommon, so swimming off the wide, sandy beach offers welcome respite.

Tsingy

In western Madagascar there are a few raised limestone plateaus eroded into unmistakable razor-sharp pinnacles the Malagasy call *tsingy*. These pinnacles range from whipped-cream peaks to the massive formations of Bemaraha, which from the air resemble thousands of church steeples crowded together. *Tsingy* is brittle, so walking in these plateaus can be hazardous and sturdy footwear is a necessity. Underneath the limestone, there are vast networks of subterranean rivers, passages and awesome caves. Accessible *tsingy* plateaus are Tsingy de Bemaraha and Ankarana. Both contain many sacred sites, burial sites, and both are home to around half the island's known bat species. Both contain 'grand tsingy' and 'petite tsingy' formations.

◀ *Left: A grove of* Adansonia madagascariensis *baobabs on limestone formations at Moramba Bay, Anjajavy. At least three of the island's six endemic baobab species are endangered. Important pollinators of their beautiful flowers include bats and hawk moths.*

Paddling Your Own Canoe

River trips along the Manambolo (three to five days, paddling) and Tsiribihina rivers (three days, motorized boat) are operated from the second half of April to late October. The Tsiribihina is easier and can be done with Espace Mada from the town Miandrivaso, where visitors can overnight at the new Lakana Hotel. The Manambolo, the more spectacular of the two, requires planning: you will need to prearrange this with your tour operator. Your journey could begin with a charter flight from Antananarivo to remote Ankavandra, where you are collected by your regional guides (Mad Cameleon arrange these adventure trips – tel: 22 63086; contact via e-mail on website: www.madcameleon.com). The trip to Bekopaka, the 'gateway' town to Tsingy de Bemaraha National Park, takes you through spectacular gorges and poorly explored deciduous forests with baobabs galore. Set aside another two full days for the park, from where it is currently a 10-hour drive south to Morondava.

Morondava ★

Arriving by plane, it is evident that there has been some planning in terms of land usage here: rice paddies and fields alternate with tracts of seasonally dry forest. Conspicuous (and impressive) from the air are thousands of giant baobabs, a tree synonymous with the Menabe.

Kirindy ★★★

What strikes people immediately about this 10,000ha (24,710-acre) forest is the sheer abundance of **baobabs**. Three of the island's endemic species are present: the largest of all, *Adansonia grandieri*, the sizeable southern species *A. za*, and smallest of all, *A. rubrostipa*. The distance from Morondava to Kirindy is about 60km (37.5 miles) along a road that is reasonable in the dry season (May to November).

Kirindy's **mammals** are its other drawcard. They include the tiniest of all primates, Madame Berthe's mouse lemur. Two larger nocturnal lemurs seldom seen elsewhere are the Coquerel's giant mouse lemur and, high up in the trees, the vociferous pale fork-marked lemur. By day you may see Verreaux's sifaka and red-fronted brown lemurs. Kirindy claims a world record for primate density in forests of comparable size. This is also the best site in which to look for the **fosa**, Madagascar's largest and most formidable carnivore. Fosa lose their fear of people during their mating season, usually in the first week of November. Females are site-faithful so return to the same mating tree annually. Some fosa also loiter around the basic camp site and rubbish dump. (They are not appreciated at villages due to their chicken-thieving prowess.) A much smaller, diurnal carnivore virtually restricted to the Menabe is the narrow-striped mongoose or *boky-boky*.

The nocturnal and critically endangered giant jumping rat is Madagascar's largest rodent: ***vozitse*** is the size of a hare and sometimes hops around the baobab forest like a little kangaroo. Like the fosa, it is best sought from November to March, just when weather is at its hottest.

◀ Left: Madame Berthe's mouse lemur is the world's smallest primate. Its stronghold is Kirindy Forest in the Menabe Protected Area.
◀◀ Opposite: The Oustalet's chameleon is the largest of all chameleons, often reaching over 65cm in length, and is common in western Madagascar.

Birds that are easily seen here include the resin-eating crested coua, the greater vasa parrot, white-headed and sickle-billed vangas, and colonies of Sakalava weaver. The greater vasa parrot – common in Kirindy – exhibits breeding behaviour unique among birds: females dominate the males and go bald in the breeding season, their heads turning orange-yellow. Males have a large phallus and mating can last for up to two hours. Up to eight males provide the incubating females and chicks with food, and females sing to solicit their attention. The parrots' preferred nesting trees are baobabs.

Kirindy is a **herpetologist**'s dream, but unfortunately most reptiles are more active during the rainy season (December–March), which is when Kirindy cannot really be visited due to hordes of horseflies, sweat-bees and murderous heat. One of the chameleons visitors are likely to see is the giant Oustalet's chameleon. The extraordinary, colourful Laborde's chameleon is found here too. Snakes are diverse and interesting.

Kirindy Practicalities

Up to now many people who have visited this forest feel their excursions have been poorly organized and this has left a bitter aftertaste. The majority of travellers will pass through the area but once in their lifetime, so **careful planning** can make all the difference. (The forest might have an exceptionally high primate density but this does not mean the animals are necessarily easy to see.)

The Madagascar Fish Eagle

Madagascar's largest raptor, the Madagascar fish eagle is one of the world's six rarest eagles. Called *ankoay* by the Malagasy, there are some 200 individuals left today. They occur from Belo-Sur-Mer to the Mitsio isles, and inland for about 100km (62 miles) along large rivers, at lakes or at the coast. *Ankoay* are a subject of research of the Peregrine Fund's Africa and Madagascar Division, which has done wonderful work for rare bird conservation in Madagascar. Almost as noisy and conspicuous as its near relative in Africa, it is duller brown in colour, with a smoky white face. *Ankoay* are sure to be seen at Ankarafantsika and at Anjajavy, where two pairs find protection at Moramba Bay. To support and learn about the Peregrine Fund's work with critically endangered Malagasy raptors, *see* www.peregrinefund.org and e-mail tpf@peregrinefund.org

▶ *Right: The red-capped coua is one of the six terrestrial members of this striking family of birds.*

Lemuria From the Sky

The ultimate way to see the best of Madagascar is by helicopter. At Marovasa-Be, Tsaranoro Valley (Andringitra Mountains), Tsarabanjina or the Masoala Peninsula, you'll be impressed by unexpected luxury in such remote, inaccessible places. Boogie Pilgrim has access to two helicopters: one for maximum three guests (max passenger weight 240kg/529 lb) and the other for four (max passenger weight 320kg/706 lb); 50kg (110 lb) luggage maximum in total for each helicopter. All departures are scheduled early morning at 08:00. Flights last from 30min to 3hrs per day, leaving plenty of time to explore dazzling beaches, spectacular national parks, interesting towns and remote countryside. In sites like Tsaranoro Valley, Salary Bay and Tsarabanjina, you may stay two to three nights to enjoy the areas. Contact Boogie Pilgrim (www.boogiepilgrim-madagascar.com) for more info. Another increasingly popular way for those who can afford it is to get around Madagascar by means of private charter flights – this means you are not dependent on domestic flight timetables.

To make the most of a visit to Kirindy, try to stay overnight. FANAMBY has set up the new Camp Amoureux near the Alley of Baoababs, with permanent, sheltered, *en-suite* tented rooms on platforms. In Kirindy itself, a basic campsite was set up in 1996 with very simple bungalows (reed and thatch) and communal ablution facilities. From about 09:00 in spring and summer mornings the **heat** is usually sweltering. Therefore, it makes sense to plan to arrive at Kirindy in the late afternoon (perhaps taking photos of the baobabs at sunset); do a night walk, stay overnight at Camp Amoureux and then make the usual early morning forest walk to take advantage of the dawn chorus. Bring **extra water** supplies.

When you are back in Morondava, you can cool off in the ocean or swimming pool. The Palissandre Côte Ouest, which currently offers the best accommodation in town, can arrange overnight excursions. But because of erratic reliability of excursion operators in Morondava, you are still best off being accompanied, in this case, by a professional wildlife guide from Antananarivo.

Tsingy de Bemaraha National Park ★★★

This enormous **World Heritage Site** covers 152,000ha (375,592 acres) and protects the largest of Madagascar's *tsingy* limestone plateaus and its associated wildlife. The *tsingy* formations are varied, with some being truly magnificent, like a bizarre forest of church steeples among which deciduous forest thrives. ANGAP/Madagascar National Parks built impressive **walkways** for the park's circuits. There are cable ropes, rocky steps, steel ladders and even a suspension bridge over one of the canyons. This is to ensure that visitors can safely explore the park without injuring themselves or damaging the brittle *tsingy* (*see* www.tsingy-madagascar.com).

The seasonally dry forests of Bemaraha contain the white Decken's sifaka, red-fronted brown lemurs, and the rarely seen western grey bamboo lemur. Two interesting nocturnal lemurs are **Cleese's woolly lemur** and the **pygmy mouse lemur**. The wildlife inventory, which no doubt will be added to, includes about 94 birds, notably the critically endangered **Madagascar fish eagle**, which has a stronghold in the Antsalova lakes region not far away. A new forest rail, *Mentocrex beankaensis*, was described from here in 2011. Among the 66 reptile species so far listed are iguanid lizards and stump-tailed chameleons. Some 22 frog species have been recorded.

This area is where the internationally cultivated '**flamboyant**' **tree** originates. There are also large, bloated and thorny pachypodium lamerei. In some caves are burial sites of the Sakalava, with open coffins on cave shelves.

Baobab Centre

Dama, the lead singer of successful Malagasy group Mahaleo, has founded a commendable initiative near Morondava, aimed at assisting impoverished migrant farmers to become self-sufficient. With access to a large tract of land, the centre is able to allocate a plot to each farmer, and teaches sustainable agricultural techniques, particularly pertaining to riziculture. Two-thirds of the produce goes to the farmers, and a third to the centre, which then builds huts and sanitation works, and installs water pumps. Visitors are invited to visit the project, where they can enjoy a delicious traditional meal and plant a baobab tree.

◀ *Left: Tsingy limestone pinnacles can be viewed in the Tsingy de Bemaraha National Park.*

Responsinble Travel: Nature Reserves

Keep to the trails in the forests to minimize the disturbance to wildlife. Do not harass wildlife and try to discourage forest guides from this practice, which unfortunately happens in a number of reserves.

Bemaraha lies in the hottest part of the country, with temperatures easily hovering around the 40°C (104°F) mark in spring and early summer. During the wet season (late November to April) the park is not accessible. The drive from Morondava – which must be done in a sturdy 4WD vehicle – takes about 10 hours, including the ferry crossing at Belo Sur Tsiribihina. Many visitors choose first to do a three-day descent of the **Tsiribihina River**, then drive north to Bekopaka, the access town to **Tsingy de Bemaraha**, and stay at the park for three nights. Break the overland journey back to Morondava with an overnight stop at Kirindy. Hotels at the park are simple.

Tsiribihina River Trips **

The wide Tsiribihina River meanders its way westwards to Belo Sur Tsiribihina on the **Mozambique Channel**. Mad Cameleon (*see* www.madcameleon.com) are currently the best at arranging the three-day descent from Masiakampy near Miandrivaso. This **river trip** will include two nights of fully equipped camping with all meals provided. Camp sites are carefully chosen on the river banks, but are rudimentary (no facilities at time of writing).

The boats are motorized, large and comfortable. Along the journey you will be taken to seldom-visited **beauty spots** such as waterfalls and tracts of deciduous forest where you may see lemurs. You will also be taken to visit **remote villages**.

Through a reliable tour operator it is possible to arrange an individual boat trip, should you prefer to have the boat to yourselves. Pack plenty of mosquito repellent, nets, and protection from the harsh sun.

▶ *Opposite: The critically endangered Madagascar fish eagle is easily seen at Lake Ravelobe in Ankarafantsika, or Moramba Bay, Anjajavy.*
▼ *Below:* Taxi-brousse *(bush taxis) are cheap and readily available but are always crowded.*

Transport: Hiring a Car

Vehicle hire is possible but more often than not people doing so have had negative experiences. (This applies even to the large, international car hire firms.) An excellent command of French would be necessary, and even then, if you are travelling through remote places, be aware that a surprisingly large proportion of rural Malagasy may not speak French. If you hire a car, you need to have mechanical skills in case of a breakdown.

Drivers can be hired, and they tend to have limited French, usually with no other European language. Drivers are not guides. In provincial areas, fuel is usually sold in plastic containers at local markets. It is imperative that your driver knows where to obtain uncontaminated fuel. Road conditions at night are often risky, with insufficient light conditions, other vehicles often not having operational lights or being roadworthy, cattle or other livestock crossing roads, and potholes.

Exercise caution when dealing directly with an operation based in Madagascar: should things go wrong, you have little or no recourse.

You can enquire about car hire companies through the Tourism Office.

SOUTH OF MORONDAVA

At the Veso village of **Belo-Sur-Mer**, large **schooners** are built, as well as pirogues. Each family specializes in making one particular length of boat, using boat-building skills that have been passed down for several generations. (A similar situation exists in the northeastern village of Manompona, where schooners are made to resemble old pirate vessels down to the finest detail, except that mainly natural materials are utilized.) Families also keep pet pigs to help dispose of garbage. Offshore are some barren, rat-infested islets surrounded by colourful **coral reefs**. The Veso sometimes use these islets as temporary bases and have constructed basic shelter out of bleached coral.

A relatively poorly explored new park near Belo-Sur-Mer is **Kirindy Mitea**. It protects large populations of three baobab species in seasonally dry forest; has two lakes protected by *fady*, mangrove and some marine habitat. At time of writing there are no facilities, so visitors should arrange fully equipped camping for an overnight stay. This needs to be reserved and carefully planned through a reputable operator to prevent the real chance of things going awry.

Best Times to Visit

Mahajanga, Anjajavy and Ampijoroa/Ankarafantsika can be visited **all year round**. Summers (December to March) are very hot with the temperature by day averaging around 32–37°C (89–98°F). Visit Morondava, Kirindy and Tsingy de Bemaraha from mid-April to early November. Tsiribihina and Manambolo River trips are operated from May to early November. (Best from mid-May to September when it is cooler.)

Getting There

Air Madagascar flies several times a week from Tana to Mahajanga and most days to Morondava. From Morondava one can fly to Tuléar (and vice versa) and from Mahajanga there are occasional flights to Nosy Bé. A private airline, Madagascar Transport Aeriens, operates three flights a week from Tana to Anjajavy return, and will, on request, arrange charters at other times to any part of the country (www.mta.mg). Roads to Mahajanga and Morondava are in good shape but scenery is rather dull.

Getting Around

Taxis are cheap and plentiful in Mahajanga and Morondava. Some hotels arrange excursions to interesting sites, but quality of transportation, food and guiding can be poor and a rip-off. Getting around Mahajanga by **rickshaw** is popular and **ferries** operate from here to Katsepy daily.

Where to Stay

Luxury

Anjajavy l'Hotel, contact@anjajavy.com bookings@anjajavylhotel.mg www.anjajavy.com Twenty-four spacious glass-fronted, thatched and air-conditioned villas. On a remote peninsula with a white sand beach, bordered by tropical dry deciduous forest, it offers luxury beach-side accommodation and wildlife in spectacular baobab forests. There's nothing else like it in the country. The villas have a double bed on ground floor and twin beds in the loft upstairs, and a hammock on the spacious veranda. Lovely pool and beach. Rates include scheduled land- and water-based activities.

La Maison de Marovasa-Be, tel: 2024 28067, contactparis@marovasabe.com charlesgassot@wanadoo.fr www.marovasabe.com Three suites, six luxury rooms, all *en suite*; restaurant and pool. Light aircraft transfers from Tana or Mahajanga. Moromba Bay lacks the forests which surround Anjajavy. Guests are invited to contribute to the local reforestation project by planting an endemic tree.

Lodges des Terres Blanches, tel: 032 05 15155, lodgeterresblanches@gmail.com www.lodgeterresblanches.com About 25km south of Anjajavy are six simple *en-suite* bungalows at a lovely beach. Guests dine together at the lodge and help themselves to drinks from the refrigerator. Wildlife in the surrounding woods. Access by light aircraft from Mahajanga airport, or by boat. Two boats for sport fishing. Picnics and hikes are arranged to secluded and beautiful, quiet coves.

Mahajanga

Luxury

Sunny Hotel, tel: 62 23587, www.sunnymada.com Forty rooms, four suites. Large restaurant serving excellent meals; enormous pool. Close to the airport, has a fitness centre, pool tables, table tennis, and they can arrange horse riding on the beach and beach volleyball.

Mid-range

Coco Lodge, tel: 62 23023, contact@cocolodge.com www.coco-lodge.com Neatly designed hotel, rooms around courtyard; sparkling pool with bar. Breakfast served only.

Le Tropicana, tel: 62 22069, hotel-tropicana@tiscali.fr Relaxed ambience; attractive garden around a pool. Good food. Simple *en-suite* rooms.

Budget

Chez Chabaud, tel: 62 23327 or 032 07 06734 (Katsepy), 032 40 53005 (Mahajanga). Eighteen rooms, some *en suite*. The legendary Chez Chabaud restaurant should be booked in advance. Run by the Chabaud sisters, daughters of the late chef Madame Chabaud. They are engaging hosts.

North of Mahajanga

Antsanitia, tel: 62 02334 032 07600, antanitia@antsanitia.com www.antsanitia.com An hour's drive from Mahajanga along a poor road, this seaside resort offers good value for money and a lovely location. Often full during Malagasy holidays.

Ankarafantsika National Park
Gîte de Ampijoroa, tel: 033 131 0286, akf.parks@gmail.com www.parcs-madagascar.com Six simple rooms with two communal bathrooms, 10 tents on platforms, and seven simple *en-suite* bungalows across the road at Lac Ravelobe. Rooms are small with comfortable beds and electric lighting but no sockets. Ablution block with cold showers. Bungalows have *en-suite* bathrooms. In the forest there is now a 'loft' comprising two rooms with a shared bathroom. The small open-air and locally run La Pigargue restaurant serves simple Malagasy meals and cold drinks. (Do inform them in advance of any special dietary requirements.) Book at least a year in advance if travelling in the peak birding months of Sep–Oct.

Morondava
Luxury
Palissandre Côte Ouest Hotel & Spa, tel: 20 95 520 522, palissandrecoteouest@gmail.com www.palissandrecote-ouest.com Four-star luxury in Morondava: beautiful luxury hotel with sparkling pool, 29 air-conditioned bungalows with satellite TV, safe, mini-bar, hair-dryer and telephone. Each bungalow has a large sea view terrace. Set in spacious grounds with coconut palms and casuarina trees. Outstanding service and good food.

Mid-range
Baobab Café, tel: 95 52012; baobabtours@blueline.mg 13 double and three twin, air-conditioned *en-suite* rooms. Good restaurant, Malagasy and continental dishes. Large pool; snooker table. They arrange excursions into the area.
Chez Maggie, tel: 95 52347, www.chezmaggie.com Eight tastefully designed bungalows and one apartment. Garden setting adjacent to the wide beach. Small pool. Good food, small bar. Excursions to Kirindy and Tsingy de Bemaraha.
Kirindy/Allee des Baobabs, tel: 032 02 12009, www.alleedesbaobabs.org Camp Amoureux is funded by FANAMBY, the Malagasy 'arm' of Conservation International, and offers permanent tented accommodation near the Alley of Baobabs, enabling night walks in Kirindy and quicker access to the forest for the dawn chorus. The camp is in Marofandila forest and is named for a pair of baobabs nearby. The seven tents are on wooden platforms with private *en-suite* bathrooms and under permanent thatch shelters. The restaurant can seat 20.

Where to Eat

Mahajanga
Chez Chabaud (for contact details *see* Where to Stay). This restaurant is regarded by many as the country's best. Book ahead.

Morondava
La Campannina, tel: 20 95 92425. Malagasy/Italian-owned, good food and attentive service.

Tours and Excursions

Morondava
The listed hotels are able to arrange excursions by 4WD to **Kirindy Forest** and **Tsingy de Bemaraha National Park**. Quality of vehicles, guiding and catering during such excursions is variable and unpredictable, especially in Morondava. For this reason it is essential to arrange travel in the Menabe through an operator so that you are accompanied by a professional, English-speaking natural history guide. This can prevent wasting precious time and make all the difference to your experience of a fascinating area. The area is seasonal; if visiting Tsingy de Bemaraha, the Grand Tsingy is accessible from June to early November only.

MAHAJANGA	J	F	M	A	M	J	J	A	S	O	N	D
AVERAGE TEMP. °C	38	35	33	31	30	30	30	30	32	33	35	37
AVERAGE TEMP. °F	100	95	91	44	88	86	86	86	90	91	95	99
RAINFALL mm	402	385	196	70	9	1	2	3	2	19	118	276
RAINFALL in	15.8	15.2	7.7	2.7	0.3	-	0.1	0.1	0.1	0.8	4.6	10.9
DAYS OF RAINFALL	20	18	16	8	1	1	1	1	1	4	10	14

5. Northern Madagascar

Fantastically varied geological formations, wildlife-rich forests and an archipelago of balmy tropical islands all contribute to the northern region's long-standing popularity with both ecotourists and beach holiday-makers. **Nosy Bé**, the largest of the offshore islands, is one of the best-known tourist destinations, thanks to a favourable climate. The far north is almost isolated by the wild, poorly explored Tsaratanana massif, which includes Madagascar's highest peak, the 2876m (9436ft) high **Mount Maromokotro**.

The beautiful **Montagne d'Ambre National Park** and the otherworldly *tsingy* plateau of **Ankarana Special Reserve** protect large populations of rare wildlife, while marine enthusiasts can explore Madagascar's best reefs around the Mitsio isles.

Diégo Suarez (Antsirañana), the region's main urban centre, is most conveniently reached by air from either Antananarivo or Nosy Bé. A dry, windy climate prevails, and scrub-covered hills surround the town. Visitors descending to the airport can see baobabs (here the regionally endemic endangered *Adansonia suarenzis*) standing like sentinels presiding over the landscape. Just 45 minutes' drive south, the climate changes abruptly at the large, isolated rainforest of Montagne d'Ambre.

Further southwest is the bizarre **Ankarana Special Reserve**, often referred to as the 'Crocodile Caves' or the 'Lost World Within a Lost World'. Ankarana is the most accessible of the island's raised limestone plateaus, decorated with fields of sharp pinnacles called *tsingy*.

Don't Miss

*** **Montagne d'Ambre National Park:** for exquisite scenery and rare wildlife.
*** **Ankarana Special Reserve:** for awesome caves, *tsingy* pinnacle-fields and wildlife.
*** **Tsarabanjina, Ankazoberavina, Iranja and surrounds:** these are arguably Madagascar's very best reefs for scuba diving.
** **Nosy Bé Archipelago:** for coral reefs, beach, water sports and island-hopping.

◀ Opposite: The Nosy Bé Archipelago is perfect for yacht charters.

Climate

Northern Madagascar's climate is diverse. Around Diégo Suarez it is generally hot, dry and quite often windy. This changes abruptly at Montagne d'Ambre, where, it is at least 6°C (11°F) cooler (cold in winter) and rainfall is high. Further southwest, Ankarana is very hot in summer with cold nights in winter. The region encapsulating Ambanja, Ankify, Nosy Komba and Nosy Bé – the 'Sambirano domain' – has a tropical climate with hot summers and very pleasant, warm winters.

The northern region can be visited year round, but rainfall can be heavy in late January to March and the heat can be stifling then.

DIÉGO SUAREZ (ANTSIRAÑANA) **

Cosmopolitan Diégo Suarez has a large natural **harbour**, with a deep bay covering approximately 250km² (100 sq miles). The colonial name stems from two Portuguese admirals, Diego Dias and Fernando Suarez, who arrived here in 1506 and caused mayhem among the local people. In 1885 the French took possession of the harbour, and in 1900 the military commander General Joseph Joffre named the nearby town of Joffreville after himself. He built forts at **Cap Diégo** and **Windsor Castle**. While the island was in the hold of the Vichy French, Cap Diego was captured by the British (1942) to prevent Japanese use of the harbour during World War II (hence the **British War Cemetery**, still visited by a steady trickle of British tourists). Diégo's population, mostly comprised of the Antakarana ('they of the harana' or 'people of the rocks') tribe, includes Arab, Indian, Chinese and Creole communities. As with most of the urban centres, Diégo has its share of aesthetically pleasing but dilapidated colonial buildings and vibrant markets. The international-standard Grand Hotel and the lovely La Note Bleue are among quality accommodations on offer.

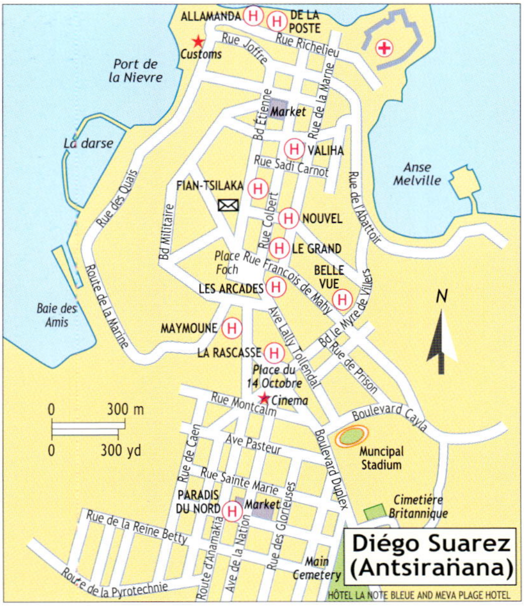

Montagne des Français *

Only 8km (5 miles) from Diégo, this dry mountain makes for a worthwhile half-day trip and is popular

▲ *Above: 'Sugarloaf' rock or Nosy Lonja in the Bay of Diégo Suarez.*

with rock-climbers. It is named to honour the Malagasy and **French casualties** suffered during the Allied invasion in 1942. This accounts for the commemorative crosses. Local flora includes baobabs and aloes. Visits should be conducted in the early morning only, due to oppressive heat. Being accompanied by a professional guide is recommended for security purposes. **Views** across the bay from here are magnificent.

Ramena Beach, Baie des Dunes and Baie des Sakalavas ★★★

About 18km (11 miles) east of town, the drive to Ramena along the bay of Diégo Suarez takes about 40 minutes. Along the way you can see the sacred island **Nosy Lonja**. The beaches of these three bays are long corridors of white sand offset by the almost emerald sea. A two-hour walk from Ramena village will take you to beautiful **Baie des Dunes**, and still further east is lovely **Baie des Sakalavas**. Swimming is safe and snorkelling is rewarding. Day excursions can be arranged through the Grand Hotel, Escapades, Cap Nord Voyages, or pre-booked through Domain de Fontenay at Joffreville.

MONTAGNE D'AMBRE NATIONAL PARK ★★★

Not far from Joffreville, 27km south of Diégo, dry savanna quickly gives way to evergreen **montane forest**. Montagne d'Ambre National Park covers about 18,200ha (45,000 acres) and protects an isolated rainforest block that is not part of the eastern rainforest band. As such, the rate of endemicity in its flora and fauna is high. Distinctive features of the massif include four **crater lakes** – the result of volcanic activity – and three much-photographed waterfalls.

Madagascar Development Fund (MDF)

The Madagascar Development Fund was founded by former British Embassy employees to replace a similar scheme that ended with the Embassy's closure. MDF received formal approval from the Malagasy authorities in July 2008. To date 63 projects have been financed throughout Madagascar, including the construction, renovation or extension of 28 state primary schools and the installation of 17 safe, clean water projects. MDF has four main areas of activity: increased access to primary education; clean water and sanitation; generating revenue for poor communities; and environmental protection.

With a well-planned system of **trails** covering about 25km (15.5 miles) and fanning out from the picnic spot Les Rousettes, Montagne d'Ambre has long been a popular **hiking** destination. Most trails are graded as easy – indeed, it is one of the few parks suitable for visitors with limited mobility – but some, such as the trail to Cascade d'Antomboka and beyond, can take half a day over some challenging terrain. At the park entrance, visitors can purchase permits, meet with local guides and obtain a comprehensive booklet about the trails, flora and wildlife. The climate in the park is markedly different to that in Diégo – it is on average at least 5°C (9°F) cooler, with higher, unpredictable rainfall. Take warmer clothing, regardless of how hot it is in Diégo.

▶ *Opposite: A field of razor-sharp, friable limestone pinnacles or* tsingy *at Ankarana Special Reserve.*
▼ *Below: Grande Cascade, in the Montagne d'Ambre National Park.*

Along the trails guides point out various **trees** with **medicinal** properties, such as the tall *ramy*, from which a cure for headaches is made, and the *famelona*, used for respiratory tract infections. Of interest to botanists is the presence of the critically endangered and large '**rainforest baobab**', *Adansonia perrieri*. You may see an enormous specimen on the trail past Cascade d'Antomboka.

Wildlife enthusiasts should see Sanford's and crowned lemurs, some of which have become well habituated. The animated northern ring-tailed mongoose or vontsira is often encountered. Birders can look out for Madagascar crested ibis, spectacled greenbul, forest rock-thrush and white-throated oxylabes among others. The park has a rich **herpetofauna**, including many species of chameleon, various leaf-tailed geckoes

(Uroplatus) and snakes. This makes night walks in the private park of Domain de Fontenay particularly rewarding, because chameleons initially reflect a ghostly white in torchlight. During such walks you can also look for the Ankarana sportive lemur and Ambre Mountain fork-marked lemur, a vocal but fast-moving, wary species that keeps high up in the trees.

The park is also usually included in the itineraries of **butterfly** fanciers.

ANKARANA SPECIAL RESERVE ★★★

The *tsingy* (limestone pinnacle) plateaus are probably the most unusual feature among Madagascar's many extraordinary natural phenomena, and Ankarana is the most accessible and best known of these, following a *National Geographic* video in the late 1980s, and

Donating to the MDF

To date MDF's activities have focused on primary education, because the majority of grant applications concern building or renovation of primary schools. There have also been grants to build healthcare facilities and a bridge. Donations made in the UK to the MDF are sent to Liverpool Charity and Voluntary Services (LCVS), a registered UK charity (No. 223485), and transferred by them to MDF's bank account in Antananarivo. On www.maddevfund.co.uk donations can be made via the Internet. Alternatively, cheques, payable to LCVS (Madagascar Development Fund), can be sent to: MDF c/o LCVS, 151 Dale Street Liverpool, L2 2AH.

▶ Right: Lac Vert is one of Ankarana's geological attractions.
▶▶ Opposite: A female crowned lemur with a youngster.

Island-hopping: Cruises into Paradise

A wonderful way of getting to know the Nosy Bé region – including the Mitsio isles, Nosy Iranja, Nosy Sakatia and the Radama isles – is a cruise on a catamaran or monohull. Reputable companies operate in the area. Their craft have *en-suite* double cabins and, usually, English-speaking crew. Diving can be organized on request. Charters often visit Baramahamay Bay, a centre of boat-building and blacksmiths. Dugout trips can be arranged up the Baramahamay River. You also visit other remote places like the dramatic basalt 'Organ Pipes' and the 'Four Brothers' rock formations. The underwater world around the four coral Radama isles – Nosy Ovy, Nosy Kalakajoro ('island of joy'), Nosy Antany Mora and the privately owned Nosy Valiha – is magnificent. Charters are usually a minimum of three nights (up to seven nights in peak season). Use of snorkelling equipment, sea kayaks and fishing rods is included in the full-board rates. Contact Escapades (www.nosybe-madagascar.com) or Bossi Island Adventures (www.bossiadventures.com), which has four catamarans: Good English spoken.

the excellent book, *Lemurs of the Lost World*, by Dr Jane Wilson.

The Special Reserve covers about 18,220ha (45,000 acres), with the fortress-like **limestone plateau** measuring roughly 5km by 20km (3 miles by 12 miles). It is about 108km (67 miles) southwest of Diégo Suarez, and the eastern sector, Ankarana Est, can be visited year round as a day excursion. To see more of the park though – including the **Grand Tsingy** formations – staying overnight at an establishment such as the new Iharana Bush Camp is recommended.

The western section – nearer to the more impressive caves (such as the spectacular **Grotte d'Andrafiabe**) and to **Lac Vert** – is more seasonal, being accessible from late May to end October. Visitors should see plenty of rare wildlife in sunken moist deciduous forests between the limestone walls and where some caves have collapsed. In subterranean rivers are underground-dwelling Nile crocodiles, blind cave fish, eels and shrimps. The caves are frequented by an abundance of bats.

By day, crowned lemurs and northern ring-tailed vontsira are easily seen. After dusk, common tenrecs, striped civets, fosa, noisy Ankarana sportive lemurs, northern mouse lemurs and at least 13 species of bat become active.

Birders may see white-breasted mesite, Madagascar harrier-hawk, greater vasa parrot, crested coua and sicklebill vanga. As is the case with many of Madagascar's protected areas, the reptile list is incomplete.

Getting To Ankarana

Ankarana can be reached from either Diégo Suarez or from Ankify via Ambanja, a frontier town around which cocoa plantations can be seen. Allow for an hour's drive from Ankify jetty to Ambanja, and then a further four hours by 4WD to the park. If coming from Ambanja, you can enter through **Mahamasina gate**, where local guides can be arranged and permits can be bought.

At the time of writing (2012) some of the basic camp sites in Ankarana – which have long-drop toilets and picnic tables and are often crowded – are in need of maintenance and litter can be problematic.

Terrain in much of the park is rugged and sturdy hiking boots are a necessity. Boardwalks have been constructed in some places to protect the brittle limestone formations. Be sure to take protective wear for the fierce tropical sun. In your daypack, take extra water as your consumption will rise dramatically in the heat. Ankarana Est – where the ***petit tsingy*** can be seen on a day excursion – is an easier option.

Marine Turtles Around Madagascar

Most plentiful of the three species known to nest around Madagascar is the large green turtle, unique amongst marine turtles in being vegetarian. Its flesh is sought-after, so it is heavily hunted. Tourists delight in seeing these turtles in the waters around Nosy Tanikely and Baobab Beach in particular. Its last stronghold near Madagascar is on the French-protected Europa Island. Annually, thousands of green turtles return to lay their eggs on the 6km (4 miles) of beaches of this inhospitable island. The smaller hawksbill turtle is also extensively persecuted in Malagasy waters, partly for its shell. The loggerhead turtle has been known to nest infrequently on the southeastern and some western beaches. The latter two species feed on marine invertebrates.

THE NOSY BÉ ARCHIPELAGO

Nosy Bé ★★

With its tropical climate and relaxed ambience, Nosy Bé is Madagascar's most developed tourist destination. There is no shortage of hotels on this island, the largest of an archipelago off the north-west coast. Nosy Bé means 'big island', and its other name, **Nosy Manitra**, 'the

perfumed isle', refers to the heady, aromatic scent of exotic crops such as vanilla, ylang-ylang and coffee. Some 280km² (110 sq miles) in size, the island's terrain is hilly, mostly featuring lush secondary tropical vegetation, but with a small tract of ***sambirano* forest** remaining at **Lokobe**.

The first settlers are thought to have arrived here in the 15th century from Africa and Arabia. An influx of Indian people influenced the architecture of the oldest settlement, **Marodoka**, and the ruins that remain may be visited today. The dominant Malagasy element in the very mixed population is Sakalava. There is also a Comorian component. In 1841 the Boina Sakalava queen, Tsiomeko, handed Nosy Bé to France, signing a treaty with Admiral De Hell, after whom Hell-Ville (Andoany), the island's 'capital', is named.

Visitors are spoilt for choice in terms of accommodation. Many hotels can organize boat excursions to the

▼ *Below: Visitors soaking up the sun on the beach at Ambataloaka, Nosy Bé.*

surrounding islands and arrange **water-based activities**, including diving, snorkelling, sailing and fishing. Only some of the hotels are at beaches suitable for bathing.

Hell-Ville is a large, **vibey coastal town** with a small harbour, lively markets and many boutiques and shops, as well as nightclubs and excellent restaurants.

The view from the top of the 329m (1079ft) **Mont Passot** makes it a suitable place at which to enjoy a sundowner while taking in the landscape, which includes seven sacred crater lakes. It is said that crocodiles in the lakes harbour the spirits of departed Sakalava and Antakarana monarchs. Further afield, one can see as far as the Mitsio Isles to the north and even to the mainland coast.

Island-hopping 2: Holidays, Hotel-based

The secret to making the most of a Nosy Bé holiday is to go island-hopping. Start with a stay on Nosy Bé at the comfortable Amporaha or Heure Bleue hotels, ideal bases for exploring Nosy Bé and for a variety of activities. Take a boat to Nosy Komba, where you can choose between the relaxed Jardin Vanille and the impeccably designed Tsara Komba. On Nosy Komba you can see black lemurs up close. End the stay with a few nights in either Constance Lodge Tsarabanjina in the remote Mitsio Isles – a cluster of six isles and some huge rock columns – which has an in-house water-sports and scuba diving centre – or at Eden Lodge at Baobab Beach, or the lovely Ankazoberavina.

Restaurants on Nosy Bé

The island's best restaurants are mostly concentrated around Ambataloaka village:

- **Chez Angeline:** Specializes in mouth-watering crab, oyster and fish dishes.
- **Karibo Restaurant:** Italian cuisine including great pizzas.

▲ *Above: Getting to the Lokobe Nature Trail at Lokobe Reserve involves a* lakana *(dugout).*

Lokobe Reserve ★★

This 740ha (1800-acre) coastal *sambirano* forest represents the last tract of original habitat left on Nosy Bé. Many endemic plants and animals are local to the reserve, outside of which is an easy and interesting **nature trail**. Half-day excursions to Lokobe are offered by the hotels, or can be pre-booked through a tour operator. Usually they involve a trip by motorized pirogue, or, if the boats are non-motorized, visitors may participate in the rowing. In the forest, you are met by your guide, who will escort you along the trail. Healthy and well-habituated black **lemurs** are commonly seen, as are nocturnal grey-backed sportive lemurs, generally found resting in tree forks. The area holds a large variety of **reptiles** and **frogs**, such as the colourful panther chameleon, which is abundant on Nosy Bé and the fat, fossorial little frog Rombophryne testudo, which spends most of its existence underground. After completing the walk, visitors are invariably taken to a local village to have a sumptuous seafood lunch.

Lokobe Nature Trails

Lokobe protects the last tract of Sambirano forest remaining on Nosy Bé. Many of the Nosy Bé hotels offer day excursions by road and by boat to the forest, where a local guide will meet you and lead you along the nature trail. You should easily see healthy black lemurs, some dozy Nosy Bé (grey-backed) sportive lemurs and colourful panther chameleons. After the walk, you will be treated to a seafood lunch, often including roasted breadfruit, crab with mango, and seafood salad at a Sakalava village.

Nosy Tanikely ★★★

This marine reserve island has long been a mecca for snorkellers, thanks to its colourful coral reefs and diverse marine life. It takes roughly an hour to walk around the island at low tide. There are dense woods and a picnic spot where hotels organizing excursions prepare meals for visitors. Tropic birds breed on the island, and Madagascar flying foxes roost in the trees. It remains a firm favourite and 'must see' for visitors to Nosy Bé.

Nosy Komba ★★

Approximately 7km (4.5 miles) from Hell-Ville, Nosy Komba, or 'island of the lemurs', is usually included with Tanikely as part of a day excursion. It has been put on the map by the flourishing population of semi-wild, endangered black lemurs behind **Ampangorina** village. These lemurs are thoroughly accustomed to visitors offering fruit. Males are jet black; the females are a rich chestnut with white ear tufts. They are known to lick certain poisonous millipedes, partly to smear their fur with the toxic saliva to rid themselves of parasites, and partly because the poison has a narcotic effect that the lemurs have come to enjoy, which explains why they may be seen lounging about in a glassy-eyed stupor at times.

On its south coast, Nosy Komba has a few lovely small beaches and **coves** where **swimming** is safe. The two best hotels are the tastefully designed Tsara Komba, and the more rustic Jardin Vanille. A two-night stay is recommended.

Missouri Botanical Gardens (MBG/MOBOT)

The mission of this extraordinary organization is 'to discover and share knowledge about plants and their environment in order to preserve and enrich life.' A resident botanist and support staff are stationed in Antananarivo.

MBG scientists are actively computerizing information on the island's 10,000 to 12,000 species of vascular plants, too many of which are still data deficient. They are preparing a Red Data Book to provide information on plants of special conservation importance. A multi-tiered botanical training program continues, with a network of local collectors working in parks and reserves.

Everything is dependent on the survival of intact tracts of forest – particularly those that protect watersheds – and with regard to gathering essential knowledge about threatened, fragile ecosystems, as well as contributing towards conservation, MOBOT is exemplary (*see* www.mobot.org).

◀ *Left: Island-hopping in a catamaran is the best way of getting to know the Nosy Bé Archipelago.*

The Assada Adventurers

Early European and British settlements on Madagascar all met disastrous ends thanks to slave-raiding by the settlers. Resultant hostility from the Malagasy, combined with malaria, wiped out most of the settlers. The last British attempt was on Nosy Bé: the 'Assada Adventurers' under Colonel Hunt arrived in 1649. The few survivors (of malaria, hostile Malagasy and brawls) fled after disillusionment and one wrote: 'I set sail from ye island of Noosa and my desire is never to see it again anymore'.

The Mitsio Isles ★★★

Situated 65km (35 miles) north of Nosy Bé, the Mitsios are a must for **scuba divers**. On the beautiful reef-ringed Tsarabanjina island, **Constance Lodge Tsarabanjina** provides luxury accommodation, impeccable service and excellent food. The lodge – one of Madagascar's finest – offers an extensive range of water- and land-based activities, including scuba diving (there is an in-house PADI dive centre) and tennis.

Some of the islands, like Nosy Ankarea, are uninhabited. **La Grand Mitsio** is inhabited by Sakalava farmers and has been affected by slash-and-burn agriculture. The rocky **Four Brothers** (Les Quatre Freres) are a haven for sea birds and a pair of the critically endangered Madagascar fish eagle.

Diving is magnificent among the **coral gardens** and drop-offs, with manta rays, gamefish, turtles, sharks and a myriad tropical fish and invertebrates present. Occasionally, whale sharks are sighted.

Nosy Saba ★★★

Some 70 miles south of Nosy Bé, opposite the seldom-explored Saramalaza Reserve, delightful Nosy Saba with its luxury eco-lodge offers the perfect location for discerning travellers to end a busy Madagascar trip. The twelve 75m² junior suites and fifteen 100m² senior suites are elegantly designed and tastefully furnished to an impeccable standard. Nosy Saba Lodge offers water-skiing, sailing, scuba diving, snorkelling, tennis and golf, along with day trips to the Radama Isles and to Saramalaza, home of the range-restricted blue-eyed black lemur. Nosy Saba is accessible by speedboat or light aircraft transfer from Nosy Bé; tel: 032 03 33302, www.nosysaba.com

▼ *Below: Aerial view of the idyllic, reef-ringed Nosy Tsarabanjina and the exclusive Constance Tsarabanjina Lodge, which has an in-house scuba diving and water-sports centre.*

Best Times to Visit

The far north and Nosy Bé Archipelago can be visited **year round** but in late January to early March rainfall, humidity and heat peak; cyclones can occur. The pleasant climate of Nosy Bé Archipelago is the main reason why it is Madagascar's most popular holiday location. Divers can benefit from the fact that there is less of a problem with visibility after the rainy season as is the case with many reefs off the Malagasy mainland.

Getting There

Air Madagascar operates regular flights to Nosy Bé (now an international airport) from Tana, Diégo Suarez and Mahajanga. It is now possible to reach Diégo by road from Tana on the **RN4** and **RN6**, but flights are only an hour or two in duration, depending on the aircraft. Nosy Bé is an established destination for visiting **yachts**. Departure points include Durban and Richards Bay in South Africa, Maputo in Mozambique and Zanzibar.

Getting Around

The 'northern circuit' on **RN6** is now just as popular as the long-established **RN7** route. Most people fly from Tana to Diégo Suarez and travel southwards overland to Ankify, via the protected areas of Montagne d'Ambre and Ankarana. From Ankify jetty, cross by **boat** to Nosy Bé, to relax on the islands for a few days, or take boat to secluded Eden Lodge for bush and beach in luxury. Transportation from Diégo to the protected areas can be arranged through a tour operator, or through certain hotels. If you do not have pre-arranged transportation in Nosy Bé, **taxis** are relatively freely available especially in Ambataloaka, a well-developed strip of beach hotels. Alternatively, hotel reception should be able to assist. Hotels can also advise you with regard to **boat** transport between the islands. Those after a live-aboard sailing experience will find some unforgettable island-hopping trips on offer. Not only do these enable access to some of the lesser-known gems in the archipelago, but you may get the chance to visit the relatively prosperous 'Sambirano' region of the remote northwest.

Where to Stay

Nosy Bé Archipelago

Luxury

Vanila Hotel, tel: 86 92101, vanilahotel@simicro.org www.vanilahotel.com Thirty-five rooms and 6 large suites. Garden or ocean views, and either air conditioned or with fan; good restaurants; efficiently managed. Good option for families; can be crowded.

Amarina Hotel, tel: 86 92128 and mobile: 032 0730747, www.amarinahotel.com Luxury rooms in remote Befotaka Bay, northern Nosy Bé (accessed by rough road). Open-air restaurant, big pool, scuba diving and water-sports centre. Suitable for family holidays. Good English spoken.

Amporaha Resort Hotel, tel: 031 02 60103, www.amporaharesort.com Recently opened, highly rated and one of the hotels of choice in Nosy Bé. Quiet location and excellent service.

Mid-range

Auberge Orangea, tel: 86 92790 or 032 04 20085, orangea@moov.mg www.orangea-nosybe.com Ten bungalows; pleasant beach. Well managed, pleasant garden with pool. Book long in advance.

Domain de Lokobe, tel: 032 2448 02, domain@nosybe-lokobe.com www.nosybe-lokobe.com Ten pleasant bungalows in beautiful surrounds. Walks in the Lokobe forest; scuba diving and water-skiing.

Heure Bleue, tel: 86 06020, resa@heurebleue.com www.heurebleue.com At the end of Ambataloaka Beach, with 11 bungalows, 8 superb new luxury chalets and an excellent restaurant with a terrace from which sunsets are unforgettable.

Nosy Komba

Luxury

Tsara Komba, tel: 032 07 440 40, resa@highspiritlodges.com www.tsarakomba.com Eight luxury bungalows utilising solar power at a small beach, and surrounded by lush woods. One of Madagascar's most stylish hotels. The owners have contributed towards development of facilities and improved living conditions for the local community. Excellent food; impeccable service.

MID-RANGE

Jardin Vanille, tel: 032 071 2797, www.Jardinvanille.com Eight wooden *en-suite* bungalows of fairly simple design linked by wooden walkway. Opposite Ankify, on the south side of Nosy Komba. The 100m² 'Tsaramanga Suite' is ideal for honeymooners, set atop boulders and the beach. Rewarding snorkelling off a cove nearby. Panther chameleons and black lemurs frequent the woods near the hotel. Good food and service.

Nosy Sakatia

This 4km-long island near Nosy Be is a centre for scuba divers, with the hotels largely catering for the diving market.

MID-RANGE

Sakatia Lodge, tel: 86 61514 or 032 07 12675. This establishment has an excellent scuba diving centre; eight bungalows. Book long in advance. Your host, José Viera, will ensure you have a great stay.

Ankazoberavina

Just 26km from Nosy Bé, this is a forested, reef-fringed island with a lovely beach and plenty of wildlife.

Ankazoberavina Ecolodge, tel: 032 0480280, ulyssesexplorer@gmail.com www.ankazoberavina.it Eight comfortable *en-suite* bungalows. Closed Jan–Mar (cyclone season). Highly recommended and enjoyed by all who have been here.

Tsarabanjina

LUXURY

Constance Lodge Tsarabanjina, tel: 034 02 152 29, lodges@constancehotels.com or resa@tsarabanjina.com 25 *en-suite* A-frame bungalows, idyllic setting. The island is exquisite and the lodge includes water- and land-based activities in its rates. Book long in advance. In April 2013 it will reopen as an all-inclusive property, following refurbishment.

Baobab Beach – Eden Lodge, tel: 034 86 93 119, mobile: 032 02 20 361, resa@edenlodge.net www.edenlodge.net/en On the mainland opposite Nosy Bé, tucked away in sambirano forest with lots of baobabs. Designed by fashion designer Frédérique Glainereau in 8ha of forest, the 8 luxury tented bungalows have *en-suite* bathrooms, their own massage tables, and a terrace overlooking the sea where turtles and dolphins are common. Access by speedboat from Ankify or Nosy Bé port.

Diégo Suarez

LUXURY

Le Grand Hotel, tel: 82 230 63. International standard hotel; 66 comfortable *en-suite*, air-conditioned rooms including four suites; restaurant with tea-room and patisserie.

Sakalava Bay (on the far side of the Ramena Peninsula)

Sakalava Bay Lodge, tel: 82 92152 informations@sakalava.com www.sakalava.com At a scenic 5km white sand beach, great for kite-surfing and windsurfing, which can be arranged at the water-sports centre. Excellent for adventurous young travellers who want to experience northern Madagascar. Simple bungalows, friendly service.

Joffreville

LUXURY

Le Domain de Fontenay, tel: 033 1134581, contact@lefontenay-madagascar.com www.lefontenay-madagascar.com Country manor with eight rooms (with lavish bathrooms) and a suite. English spoken. Transfers from Diégo airport and excursions to places like Montagne d'Ambre; Ankarana Est (all year); the fragile Tsingy Rouge formations; Windsor Castle and the north coast bays. Tides depending, they can take you to Ambolobozokely, an island with a baobab grove and fishing village. The lodge has a 300ha private reserve, in which day and night walks are offered; the owners are hard at work reforesting degraded areas.

Litchi Tree, tel: 33 12 784 54, thelitchitree@hotmail.com www.thelitchitree.com The villa was thoughtfully renovated in 2008. Excellent service and food. Beautiful views as far as Diego Suarez, and the hotel is closest to the park entrance.

MID-RANGE

Nature Lodge, tel: 032 071 2306, naturelodge:@

wanadoo.mg www.naturelodge-ambre.com Ten comfortable wooden bungalows, neat restaurant and bar; good food and friendly service. Book long in advance, especially for the September to November peak wildlife-watching months.

Ankarana

Mid-range

Iharaña Bush Camp, www.Iharanabushcamp.com Tasteful accommodation at Ankarana Ouest, accessible from May to early November. The camp is close to the park gates and has 8 *en-suite* bungalows largely built using local materials. Bungalows are split levels with bathrooms downstairs and bedroom upstairs. Kerosene lamps only, so take a strong torch. Fine views of Ankarana Ouest and a lake from the camp. Best visited mid-May to early November.

Le Relais de l'Ankarana (at Ankarana Est), tel: 032 02 222 94, ankarana.lerelais@gmail.com www.relaisdelankarana.unblog.fr Small, well-run lodge at Mahamasina, 30km north of Ambilobe, ideal if you want to see Ankarana Est. (A few minutes' walk from park entrance.) There's running water and solar power; electricity is supplied from 18:00–22:00 daily.

Tsingy Lodge, tel: 082 22599, info@kingdelapiste.com www.kingdelapiste.de This lodge, 1km from the eastern entrance of Ankarana Special Reserve, is surrounded by limestone and woods with prolific wildlife, particularly nocturnal animals.

Tours and Excursions

While Montagne d'Ambre is easy to get to and close to three good lodges, Ankarana remains a place to where travel should be carefully planned. You need to be accompanied by a guide.

Le King de la Piste, York and Lydia Pareik, tel/fax: 82 25599, infoking@wanadoo.mg They have Range Rovers and Mercedes unimogs. It's expensive, but they are able to arrange trips to remote places like Analamera Reserve (home to the critically endangered all-black Perrier's sifaka) and Cap d'Ambre. They also run Tsingy Lodge at Ankarana Est; it is at its best when York is present.

Cap Nord Voyages, tel: 032 07666, cap.nord.voyages@wanadoo.mg www.cap-nord-voyages.com Recommended for trips such as Ankarana, where guiding and good organization are essential.

Escapades (tel: 261 033 12 126 24, www.nosybe-madagascar.com) offer sailing trips in catamarans for individuals and small private groups. Book well in advance for live-aboard catamaran trips from 3–7 days, and visit islands such as the Mitsios (north), Radama islands (south) and other remote sites in this balmy archipelago.

Useful Contacts

Nosy Bé

Arts Madagascar, Ave de l'Indépendance, Hell-Ville, and **Chez Abud** (essential oils, perfume, clothing); these are worth a visit.

Pharmacies Tsarajoro and **Nouroudine** in Hell-Ville are reliable; an after-hours service is alternated between the two.

Pharmacy Toko Toko, tel: 86 92782 is the best pharmacy.

Espace Medical Care, tel: 86 92599 or 032 04 43115, provides good medical care.

BNI Bank (Credit Lyonnais) will arrange cash advances on Visa card; open Mon–Fri, 08:30–15:00.

Antsirañana

Regional Tourist Office (ORTDIS), tel: 82 91799, info@office-tourisme-diego-suarez.com www.office-tourisme-diego-suarez.com

All major banks have branches in town (BFV, BMOI, BNI, BOA), many with ATMs and Western Union facility.

DIÉGO SUAREZ	J	F	M	A	M	J	J	A	S	O	N	D
AVERAGE TEMP. °C	32	30	30	28	27	26	26	27	30	32	32	32
AVERAGE TEMP. °F	90	86	86	82	81	79	79	81	86	90	90	90
RAINFALL mm	338	306	179	52	13	19	19	19	9	17	55	171
RAINFALL in	13.3	12.1	7.1	2.1	0.5	0.8	0.7	0.7	0.4	0.7	2.2	6.7
DAYS OF RAINFALL	14	11	12	4	3	3	3	3	2	5	5	14

6. Eastern Madagascar

The verdant east is widely appreciated for its **rainforest band**, in which impressive protected areas beckon nature enthusiasts. One of the island's most visited holiday venues, **Ile Sainte Marie** (also an internationally rated whale-watching site), lies off the east coast. Some of Madagascar's chief export crops – coffee, cloves, vanilla and lychees – are grown here.

The **Betsimisaraka** – Madagascar's second-largest tribe – occupy much of the region. Around Lake Alaotra in the northern central east live the **Sihanaka** ('people of the swamps'), and Moramanga in the central eastern escarpment is a centre of the **Bezanozano** tribe. It is a little more complicated in the southeast, where there are a number of tribes in a fairly small portion of the country.

When planning your itinerary, note that this region receives rain all year long, and try to avoid visiting from late January to early March, as cyclones occur at this time during most years. Seek local advice when venturing out to swim, snorkel or dive, because **sharks** are common. There are wonderful reef-protected coves on the western sides of Ile Ste Marie and the great **Masoala National Park**.

Don't Miss

***** Analamazaotra ('Perinet') and Mantadia:** abundant wildlife in three protected rainforests.

***** Masoala National Park:** magnificent rainforest, wildlife and rainforest trails.

***** Ste Marie:** relaxing sea, sun and sand holidays; whale-watching

***** Pangalanes Canal, Lac Ampitabe and Vohibola:** boat trips and planting a tree.

**** Marojejy National Park:** trekking, rugged scenery and wildlife.

◀ *Opposite: An aerial view of the Pangalanes Canal shows its proximity to the Indian Ocean.*

ANTANANARIVO TO TAMATAVE

Andasibe-Mantadia National Park and Analamazaotra Forest Station ★★★

Three hours east of Tana by the excellent RN2 road is the village of **Andasibe**, around which a number of currently separated rainforest and marsh sites are located.

▶ *Right: Visitor on a trail in Analamazaotra (Périnet) Special Reserve, Andasibe-Mantadia National Park.*

These lie within the extensive **Mantadia-Vohidrazana rainforest block** and include the unprotected **Maromizaha** ('Dragon tree') rainforest, the 10,000ha (24,710-acre) **Mantadia National Park**, **Analamazaotra Forest Station**, **Analamazaotra Special Reserve**, **Torotorofotsy Marsh** and **Vohimana**. There are five lodges – the comfortable Vakona Forest Lodge, Andasibe Hotel, airy Eulophiella, basic Feon'ny ala, and small, simple Grace Lodge. Ideally, two or three nights should be spent here, which will allow time for morning walks in Analamazaotra Special Reserve and Forest Station; visit Mantadia National Park, and make a night walk in Analamazaotra Forest Station.

Many people refer to Analamazaotra Special Reserve as **Périnet**, the name of the railway station at Andasibe village.

Analamazaotra (Périnet) Special Reserve ★★★

Situated about 145km (90 miles) east of Tana, this 810ha (2001-acre) tract of mid-altitude **montane rainforest** is Madagascar's most visited rainforest, largely due to its accessibility and varied rainforest wildlife, notably two well-habituated groups of indri.

Roughly the size of a large baboon, **indri** can only be seen in its natural habitat as it does not survive in captivity due to a specialized diet of leaves from endemic forest trees. Its eerie, siren-like wailing cry is the hallmark sound of Madagascar and can carry for 3km (2 miles) across the rainforest. The Malagasy call indri *babakoto* – the 'dog-headed man' – because of its appearance and size. Walking towards the rainforest at dawn and hearing the indris calling is Malagasy magic at its best. Other resident **lemurs** are the shy eastern lesser bamboo lemur and common brown lemur. Night walks usually reveal eastern avahi, weasel sportive lemur, Goodman's mouse lemur, and in the summer, furry-eared dwarf lemur. Analamazaotra is included in all **birding** itineraries. Among its avian denizens are Madagascar wood-rail, Madagascar flufftail, red-fronted and blue couas, common sunbird-asity and nuthatch vanga. The Special Reserve claims a world record for number of **frog species** among comparably sized rainforests, but unfortunately its reptile fauna has suffered due to poaching for the exotic animal trade. Altitude in the reserve ranges from 900–1250m (2953–4101ft) and the well-maintained trails are graded as easy. The approximately 30-strong cadre of local guides known as **Association des Guides d'Andasibe** is highly skilled and knowledgeable.

CLIMATE

Eastern Madagascar's rainfall is very high, increasing from south to north and peaking around Maroantsetra with an average of 3500–5000mm (138–197 in) per year. Rain falls on 300–320 days of the year but mostly at night. Dry months with hot, sunny weather are from August to November. Violent cyclones strike during late January to March. Humidity is high. Temperatures are lower on the escarpment where winter nights are cold.

◀ *Left: The eastern lesser bamboo lemur is frequently seen in Analamazaotra Special Reserve.*

Preparing for the Future: Association Mitsinjo

Fikambanana Mitsinjo is doing brilliant work around Andasibe. They manage the 700ha (1730-acre) Analamazaotra Forest Station (across the road from Analamazaotra Special Reserve) as an ecotourism concession. There is a habituated group of indri and rich reptile fauna. This is where Andasibe-Mantadia visitors come to experience the rainforest at night. Through Mitsinjo you can also arrange trekking visits to Torotorofotsy Marsh, a stronghold of some very rare wildlife, including the iconic golden mantella frog, the extremely elusive slender-billed flufftail and critically endangered greater bamboo lemur. Tourism-generated funds are used for education and health programmes in the local community. According to Dr Rainer Dolch, ecotourism only truly works where the money it generates is used for projects with direct bearing on the lives of people living around vulnerable habitats. Mitsinjo has more than one tree nursery, where about 100 tree species are cultivated: forest corridors are being created to link isolated rainforest blocks, and severely degraded land is being rehabilitated (e-mail: mitsinjo@hotmail.com and see www.mitsinjo.org).

Analamazaotra Forest Station ★★★

Managed by proactive NGO Fikambanana (Association) Mitsinjo as an ecotourism concession, this rainforest is an extremely inspiring place to explore. This is where visitors who would like to experience the rainforest environment at night are welcome.

It is a rewarding site for a variety of chameleons and leaf-tailed geckoes and shares the same lemur species with the Special Reserve. Here you can also have the gratifying experience of literally 'putting something back', by planting an endemic tree from Association Mitsinjo's nurseries.

The NGO employs about 100 people and revenue generated by tourism is used for the upliftment of communities living around intact habitat. It is a fine example of local people directly benefiting from **ecotourism**. So far over 1 million trees have been planted to create forest corridors.

Marais de Torotorofotsy ★

At 1000ha (2471 acres) this was the largest and most intact **marsh** in eastern Madagascar. A considerably larger portion of the site is made up of degraded rainforest. The marsh flora is dominated by coarse sedges and rushes, bordered in places by ericoid scrub peppered with Pandanus. This **Ramsar Site** and **IBA** (Important Bird Area) is the main locality for Madagascar's flagship frog, the brightly coloured **golden mantella**. Birders come here to look for the island's most enigmatic bird, the slender-billed flufftail, of which the unusual call was first recorded by ornithologist Lucienne Wilmé. Of great interest to lemur-watchers is the recent discovery of a population of **greater bamboo lemur**. Association Mitsinjo – which also has excellent and personable guides – are the people to contact about excursions to the marsh. Unfortunately, the marsh was severely degraded by draining and fires during the last two years.

Mantadia National Park ★★★

About 37km (23 miles) north of Andasibe by dirt road, Mantadia allows visitors the chance to experience primary rainforest, and to see **wildlife** such as the attractive diadem sifaka and black-and-white ruffed lemur, as well as a plethora of rare rainforest birds and reptiles. Lucky **birders** may see all four of the rainforest-dependent ground-rollers, including the island's most attractive bird, the pitta-like ground-roller. The **scenery** is breathtaking inside the forest and from viewpoints along the high ridges. Mantadia has a well-mapped network of **trails**, though these are narrower than in Périnet and slopes are steeper. Terrain can be slippery during or after rain and sturdy footwear is a requirement. If the road to the park is rendered impassable, you might wish to visit Marohizaha or Vohimana instead.

Vohimana ★★

Adventurous travellers would enjoy this 800ha (1977-acre) rainforest site, which ranges from 700–1040m (2297–3412ft) in altitude and is managed by the small NGO MATE (Man And The Environment). Specializing in ethnobotany, MATE has established a **nursery** and built a **distillery**, the aim of which is to demonstrate that **biodiversity** can be conserved without the displacement of local people.

◀ *Left: The rainforest at Vohimana holds an astonishing variety of endemic reptiles (especially chameleons) and frogs, and is especially rewarding for night walks.*

The World's Rarest Duck: A Sensational Rediscovery

The Madagascar pochard or *onjy* was last seen at Lac Alaotra in 1973. Extensive searches since then by ornithologists Mark Pidgeon and Lucienne Wilmé failed to locate one, until hunters brought a live male to Wilmé in late 1991. Unfortunately it perished before another could be procured. No trace of the pochard was found and it was presumed extinct until the sensational discovery in 2006 of a thriving population of at least 10 pairs by the Peregrine Fund's Madagascar programme director Lily-Arison Rene de Roland. The birds frequent two remote, forest-encircled volcanic lakes in northern Madagascar, and are being monitored by the Wildfowl & Wetlands Trust (WWT) and the DWCT. For more information on the very successful project which has more than doubled the population of the world's rarest duck, *see* www.wwt.org.uk/our-work/wetland-wildlife/madagascar-pochard/wwt-team-pochard-blog

▶ *Right: A colourful market in Moramanga.*

Plant an Endangered Tree!

The inspiring NGOs Association Mitsinjo and MATE (Man And The Environment) both have extensive tree nurseries, offering visitors the chance of literally putting something back into Madagascar, by planting an indigenous tree. Vohimana, a delightful rainforest full of lemurs, chameleons and frogs, is near Analamazaotra. Here, MATE has simple lodging, a distillery for essential oils, and a tree nursery. They work to implement alternative, sustainable methods of forest management. Specialist tour operators can get involved from abroad, too: in 2006, UK-based Rainbow Tours' donation to the Small Grants Scheme (FAP) financed, among other things, the construction of a new classroom in the village of Ambavanalasy at Vohimana. MATE are also working at Vohibola in the Pangalanes Canal area to conserve a rare example of east coast littoral forest (*see* www.mate.mg).

In the nursery 120 tree species are cultivated. The saplings are used to create a **forest corridor** linking Vohimana, Mantadia and Vohidrazana. Along enjoyable hiking trails you may see indri, groups of diadem sifaka and brown lemurs. Trail grading is generally moderate. Bird life is similar to that of Analamazaotra. **Night walks** are exceptionally rewarding, because chameleons and frogs (some 80 species) are still plentiful. There are some basic bungalows, a house for researchers, and a dormitory on a steep slope; communal ablution facilities, and a dining area with fireplace where delicious meals are taken around a large table. From here, the **view** over the forested gorge is one of the most picturesque anywhere in Madagascar. There is also a roosting site for four Malagasy bat species in the remains of the 1905 rail tunnel.

Moramanga

A large, lively town situated 30km (20 miles) from Analamazaotra along both the railway and the road, Moramanga is historically significant to the Malagasy because a number of people were killed here in the 1947 uprising. Avoid eating at restaurants in this town due to the large number of incidents of food poisoning.

Lac Alaotra ★

Madagascar's biggest lake, Alaotra, which is 40km (25 miles) long, is now only 30% of its original size due to siltation following deforestation around it. This is where music producer, leading expert on Malagasy music and fellow of the Anglo-Malagasy Society, **Paddy Bush**, made the fascinating documentary film *Like A God When He Plays*, about Malagasy musical legend Rakotozafy. The film shows Bush attending the ***Famadihana*** (exhumation ceremony) of his musical hero. Around the lake live the Sihanaka people, and in reed beds and papyrus fringes is found the critically endangered Alaotra reed lemur, chosen by the Durrell Wildlife Conservation Trust for their SAFE (Saving Species From Extinction) projects. In 2010 a critically endangered carnivore, Durrell's vontsira, was described from the lake. The lake can be reached by variable road to Ambatondrazaka (approximately seven hours' drive time) and is for **adventurous** travellers with a **cultural** interest.

Camp Bandro, Andreba

From Ambatondrazaka, a 45-minute drive takes adventurous travellers to Andreba. Camp Bandro has two twin rooms and camping space. A local chef buys your food and cooks meals. To see the Alaotra gentle/reed lemurs and birds, take a guided canoe tour on the lake and into the Bandro Park (about two hours; maximum two persons per canoe). Sunrise on Lake Alaotra is magically surreal. Park entry fees go to the community association. For useful information and to find out more about Andreba, subscribe to the excellent online journal Madagascar Conservation & Development (MCD) by visiting www.mwc-info.net/en/services/journal.htm

The Pangalanes Canal ★★

This 600km (370-mile) chain of waterways and man-made lakes runs roughly parallel to the east coast, from Port Fluvial (the Tamatave harbour), almost down to Vangaindrano. It was once used as an alternative to the rough seas, but then became overgrown.

◀ *Left: A Three Horses Beer truck crossing the Pangalanes Canal on a raft.*

Most Visited Protected Areas

According to figures released in May 2012 by Madagascar National Parks, 159,129 people visited the state-run protected areas in 2011. The most popular national park, Isalo, attracted 32,714 visitors. In second place, Andasibe-Mantadia had 26,054 visitors while in third place, Ranomafana – which usually has more scientists than tourists and where good accommodation is in seriously short supply – had 21,775. This was followed closely by the marine reserve Nosy Tanikely, with 21,692 tourists. Three other parks had over 10,000 visitors: Montagne d'Ambre (14,977), Ankarana (13,719) and, surprisingly, the remote Tsingy de Bemaraha (10,093).

Much of the obstructing vegetation has been cleared almost as far south as Mananjary. Two hotels, Le Palmarium and the Bush House, are near the **Akanin'ny Nofy village** ('the nest of dreams') at the tranquil **Lac Ampitabe**. The hotels are reached by means of motorized boat transfers from Manambato village. From here the boat ride is about an hour. The Palmarium has spacious, comfortable *en-suite* bungalows and a good restaurant. Semi-wild lemurs, which live in the 60ha (148-acre) east coast **littoral forest reserve** at the back of the hotel, are delightful, entertaining guests by raiding breakfast tables and swinging on rafters or light cables.

Besides the various lemur species present in the reserve, you can also see interesting plants such as the sole Malagasy cactus (an epiphyte) and both the island's pitcher plants. Reptiles and frogs abound.

An enjoyable excursion on offer is to **Vohibola**, a rare example of east coast littoral forest, which protects certain critically endangered endemic trees. Guests are encouraged to plant an endemic tree from the nursery, thereby making a valuable contribution to conservation through tourism.

TAMATAVE AND SURROUNDS

Tamatave (Toamasina) is Madagascar's main port. Its Malagasy name means 'it is salty', a comment allegedly made by the Merina king Radama I on tasting the water. Formerly a **pirate base**, Tamatave attracted the attention of the French in the late 1700s, and **Napoleon** sent Sylvain Roux there to establish a foothold.

In 1811, however, Sir Robert Farquhar organized a naval squadron to attack the French, with the intention of stopping the slave trade. The French residents were exiled and the Brits remained in Tamatave, strengthening trade between Madagascar and Mauritius. Tamatave's location relative to Mauritius meant that it soon became the country's chief trading port, and the RN2 road from Tamatave to Tana remains Madagascar's most important route.

Tamatave (Toamasina)

With its wide streets and boulevards, Tamatave is a fairly pleasant city. The weather can be oppressive due to high humidity and tropical heat. There are a few good restaurants, cafés and reasonable hotels. Most visitors do not stay longer than a night, as it is usually a stopover on the way to or from Ste Marie, Maroantsetra or the Pangalanes Canal.

▼ *Below: View of the Bush House, a relaxed hotel at Lac Ampitabe which is part of the chain of waterways that make up the Pangalanes Canal.*

Those with a day on their hands should visit **Parc Ivoloina**, which has a successful lemur breeding and rehabilitation project funded by the **Madagascar Fauna Group** (*see* www.savethelemur.org). The species in focus is the vociferous, rainforest-dependent black-and-white ruffed lemur. They are slowly being reintroduced into **Betampona Reserve**, an isolated and threatened rainforest tract in a severely degraded landscape. Ivoloina is 12km (7.5 miles) north of Tamatave and in the surrounding woods there is a fair amount of wildlife. Free-ranging lemurs include the ruffed, red-bellied and white-fronted lemurs. Of note is an inspiring **environmental education centre**.

Conservation-Orientated Whale-Watching

Humpback whales are a huge (no pun intended) attraction around Ste Marie and Antongil Bay – where they stay from early July to mid-September every year. Various St Marian hotels offer conservation-orientated whale-watching excursions during these months. This gives visitors the chance to join the MEGAPTERA whale-specialist team, and gain a deeper insight into the complex lives of these extraordinary marine giants, as well as helping the team to collect some scientific data. *See* www.megaptera.org for information, photographs and recent annual reports.

STE MARIE ISLAND (NOSY BORAHA)

This long, narrow island off the east coast is one of the country's premier holiday destinations. Along its reef-protected west coast, especially, are mostly small to medium-sized, unobtrusive hotels offering a variety of water- and land-based activities. It has, like the Mitsio Isles of the Nosy Bé Archipelago, the ambience of a classical Indian Ocean **paradise**, with white coves overhung by coconut palms and bordered by coral formations. The Ste Marians – many of whom have French names – consider themselves to be a separate tribe.

In the late 1600s, Ste Marie was a prominent pirate base, frequented by infamous seafaring hooligans such as William Kidd and Thomas White. Ste Marie was the first part of Madagascar obtained by France when Princess Bety, who had married a French pirate, Jean-Onesime Filet (*La Bigorne*), handed the island over to France. The island had originally been a wedding gift from her father, the Betsimisaraka king Ratsimilaho, son of a Betsimisaraka woman and the pirate Thomas White.

Ste Marie has the world's only **pirate cemetery**, with graves dating back to the 1830s. Situated between Baie des Forbans and the village of Mahavelo, it is accessible by foot at low tide. In the **Baie des Forbans** is **Ilot Madame**, a small offshore island which was once a centre of the French East India Company.

The island is readily accessible by means of regular flights from Tana and/or Tamatave. Air Madagascar flies to Ste Marie most days but it is a good idea to check the latest schedules to make absolutely certain. Flights and the better hotels tend to be heavily booked from July to September (whale-watching season), so book well in advance. The little airport is near the southern tip of the island and many hotels have vehicles waiting for guests as the flights arrive.

Ambodifotatra is the main town and there are a great many small villages with tiny wood, bamboo and palm-thatch houses constructed on stilts. There are few roads. Most of the Ste Marian hotels hire out **bicycles** and this is the best way (and the most fun) to get around the island.

◀ Opposite: Every year from July to late September hump-back whales are a major drawcard for Ile Ste Marie and Antongil Bay. Princesse Bora Lodge in particular offers unforgettable whale-watching excursions.

▼ Below: The stylish Princesse Bora Lodge offers the best accommodation on Ste Marie Island.

Tsiny

If you see a tree, rock or water source fenced off, and possibly pieces of white cloth tied to a pole or branch, you may be looking at the dwelling of a *tsiny*: the *tsiny* are nature spirits inhabiting specific locations, such as trees, streams or rocks. The *tsiny* mediums are guardians or caretakers of these spirits and of their abodes. Periodically, they are possessed by the *tsiny*, but this is not done in public, like the Sakalava *tromba* are. Because a *tsiny*'s home is sacred, people must request permission from the local medium to leave offerings for the spirit at its haunt. *Tsiny* homes (and those of their mediums) are usually in small villages or out in the countryside.

Other than **whale-watching**, activities offered by hotels include **mountain biking**, **snorkelling** and **scuba diving** (especially wreck diving, which can be arranged through the scuba diving centre Lemurien Palme: www.lemurien-palme.com). Guests of the superb Princesse Bora Lodge have the chance to contribute towards the conservation of humpback whales by gathering data during the excursions, which are accompanied and regulated by a specialist. In whale-watching season, Princesse Bora whale-watching trips cost €90 per person (now payable locally). Ste Marie and the delightful satellite isle of Ile Aux Nattes (Nosy Nato) are included in the itineraries of orchid enthusiasts: aside from impressive Angraecoid and Aeranthes species (among many others), Nosy Nato is a site for the rare and massive 'La Grande Orchidee Rose', a spectacular plant which co-habits with certain species of Pandanus.

MAROANTSETRA AND THE MASOALA PENINSULA

Remote Maroantsetra acts as a gateway to the Masoala Peninsula, which has Madagascar's largest remaining **lowland rainforest** and **largest national park**. Because of rough terrain and a rainy climate (up to 6000mm/236in per annum), the Masoala is sparsely inhabited and has no roads. The rainforest is part of the World Heritage Site of the Atsinanana rainforests, recently placed on the danger list due to illegal logging.

▼ *Below: A canal scene in Maroantsetra, the gateway town to Masoala National Park and Nosy Mangabe.*

◀ *Left: The fringed gecko* (Uroplatus) *is easily seen on Nosy Mangabe where it thrives in the relative absence of predators.*

Scenically, it is arguably without equal in places, and this, combined with its natural assets, mark it out as the **most sought-after** destination in the northeast.

Maroantsetra ★

Strolling around this relaxed town one cannot help but wonder how such a sizeable settlement could have been built in so remote a locality. The town is spread along the banks of a network of canals and has a surprising number of shops and an interesting market. The **Relais du Masoala**, with its 15 spacious *en-suite* bungalows and pool, provides excellent accommodation and can arrange boat transfers to the lodges on the west coast of the Masoala Peninsula, excursions to Nosy Mangabe and even (expensive) boat trips to Mananara, for people who are absolutely determined to see wild aye ayes.

Nosy Mangabe ★★★

About 5km (3 miles) from Maroantsetra in the deep, blue **Antongil Bay**, this rainforest-clad, uninhabited 520ha (1285-acre) reserve island was set up primarily with **lemur conservation** in mind. In combination with Masoala

Captain William Kidd

In 1695 a commission under William III granted William Kidd authority to loot any ships he encountered. Kidd and his gang of cut-throats began plundering in the western Indian Ocean, settling eventually on Ste Marie, the greatest pirate stronghold the world had ever known. On returning to America they were arrested because the British East India Company had embarked on an anti-piracy campaign. They were hanged in London.

▲ *Above: The great Masoala rainforest still extends unbroken down to the Bay of Antongil in many places.*

National Park, Nosy Mangabe can offer a truly unforgettable wildlife experience. The island has steep slopes, which are slippery after rain. Boats land at a small beach.

By day, black-and-white ruffed and white-fronted lemurs are quite easily seen. The main reptile attraction is the **fringed gecko**, which thrives here in the relative absence of predators. (Sadly, many have been poached for the illegal exotic animal trade.) It is one of the world's biggest geckoes and has in excess of 300 teeth. Because of its outrageous appearance, this master of camouflage is associated with evil forces by some Malagasy. Another bizarre-looking denizen of Nosy Mangabe – and one surrounded by even more local beliefs because of its appearance – is the **aye aye**. Decades ago, when their continued existence was considered doubtful, a few were released here. Although they flourish, most visitors do not see them: at the size of an overgrown house cat, aye ayes are large animals but they move quickly and quietly, and emerge only at dusk. Other wildlife includes a profusion of chameleons and frogs, such as the elegant little climbing (green-backed) mantella.

Masoala Practicalities

Independent travel to this stunningly beautiful national park is challenging. Climate is an important consideration: weather is best from September to mid-December, but in July–September fantastic whale-watching is to be had. Aside from its incredible rainforest, Masoala also protects three marine reserves (10,000ha/ 24,710 acres) which contain extensive coral reefs and healthy mangroves. A useful website for those investigating Masoala is www.masoala.org Here, adventure travellers can find information about challenging trekking circuits, the mountain bike journey from the vanilla town Antalaha down to Cap Masoala, and you can also learn about *fady* adhered to in the region.

MASOALA NATIONAL PARK ★★★

The spectacle created by lowland rainforest meeting the blue waters of Antongil Bay is truly unforgettable.

The higher reaches of the peninsula's mountain chains are often covered in a cloud mantle, giving it a brooding effect. Gin clear **rivers** and **streams** run their course into the bay, and in discrete coves are some unspoilt coral formations. One of the largest of the country's national parks at 230,000ha (568,330 acres), Masoala is thought to contain a higher **biodiversity** than any other of the national parks.

Lohatrozona and Tampolo ★★★

About halfway down the west side of the peninsula, this is an area of outstanding natural beauty. It can be reached only by boat, which takes around 90–120 minutes from Maroantsetra. Sea conditions become rough from about midday, so boat transfers are generally operated only until about 10:00. There is a system of **trails** – particularly rewarding near **Arrollodge** – which can mostly be completed as half-day walks. Slopes are very steep in places and trails can be narrow and slippery. Take a small umbrella in your day pack in the event of a sudden downpour.

Currently there are three lodges in the vicinity of **Tampolo Marine Reserve** and the **Lohatrozona rainforest**. Activities on offer include guided rainforest **walks** (day and night), **sea kayaking**, **snorkelling**, **boat trips** and visits to a **Betsimisaraka village**. From July to end September humpback whales are often seen in **Antongil Bay**, as are dolphins, porpoises, feeding frenzies of game fish and delicate, iridescent flying fish.

The robust red-ruffed lemur is local to Masoala and several other lemurs, such as aye aye and the resin-

◀ Left: The helmet vanga is an icon of the northeastern rainforest national parks of Masoala and Marojejy. It uses its blue beak to deal with prey such as large stick insects.

Saving Madagascar's Frogs

With around 500 species, Madagascar has a spectacular frog fauna. But due to habitat loss and overexploitation for the pet/exotic animal trade, some frogs, such as the brightly coloured golden and harlequin mantellas, are now on the edge of extinction. The recently conceived ACSAM Iniative (A Conservation Strategy for the Amphibians of Madagascar) is the first programme to tackle the conservation of such a diverse frog fauna. According to expert Dr Franco Andreone, it may well become a model for a global amphibian conservation strategy. Dr Andreone emphasizes that we should aim to conserve not just large tropical forests, but also the small parcels of natural habitat we still have right on our doorsteps. Protecting a small pond and the vegetation around it can contribute significantly towards conservation of amphibians. Donations to the Amphibian Specialist Group and associate programmes will help to fund field surveys and the purchase of small parcels of habitat where the most threatened frogs live. See www.sahanogasy.org or www.francoandreone.it for more information.

Scuba Diving off Ste Marie

The coral formations around Ste Marie include some excellent dive sites. Wreck diving is an added bonus.
Run by capable instructors, the Lemurien Palme scuba diving centre arranges diving excursions as well as scuba diving courses for beginners, who can obtain an international diving license here. For more information, see www.lemurien-palme.com

munching fork-marked lemur, exist here. The rarely seen **fanaloka**, which looks something like the cross between a strange fox and a weasel, inhabits marshy areas where it lives almost entirely on invertebrates. Streaked **tenrecs** are common. When irked, they raise their spines and will stand their ground. Fist-sized and aptly named, the tomato frog should not be handled as the white substance it secretes can cause an allergic reaction on human skin. A sizeable proportion of visitors to the park are **birders**, who come mostly to add the helmet vanga to their check lists. Other commonly seen species include red-breasted coua and scaly ground-roller. The park is a stronghold for three very rare endemics – the **Madagascar serpent eagle**, **Madagascar red owl** and **Bernier's vanga**.

Local flora includes the forest coconut or ***voaniaola***, a rare palm confined to primary rainforest.

The best time to visit Masoala is from September to mid-December. In March the weather becomes miserable fairly abruptly, with incessant rain and winds. Flight schedules and logistics involved in getting around the Masoala mean visitors should set aside four or five days for this wonderful place.

SAMBAVA

Sambava is the centre of one of Madagascar's export mainstays, **vanilla**. Most of it is exported to America for use in ice cream. Interestingly, the vanilla orchid, an introduction from Mexico, is pollinated by hand because its natural pollinator has not been introduced.

Part of the northeastern 'SAVA' region, Sambava has white sand beaches but very strong cross currents so swimming is not advised. Visitors can arrange to visit a vanilla factory.

▼ Below: The best-known frog of the northeast is the poisonous tomato frog, seen around Maroantsetra.

MAROJEJY NATIONAL PARK ★★

Currently this rugged part of the Atsinanana rainforests **World Heritage Site** is able to cater only for small numbers of visitors – about 17 – at a time. Physical fitness and almost expedition-level preparation are necessary because reaching the park is time-consuming. The terrain is **challenging**, being graded as difficult by Hilary Bradt and Nick Garbutt, two British Madagascar experts who produced a lot of publicity for this wonderful park. The park was put on the tourist map largely by Eric Mathieu (who runs the site www.marojejy.com) and by lemur expert and international authority on the critically endangered silky sifaka, Erik Patel (*see* www.simpona.com).

From Sambava you take a pleasant hour's drive inland along the excellent tarmac road to Andapa, and enthusiastic hikers may leave their vehicles and start their walk to the park at **Manentenina village**. You will pass by cultivated plots, rice paddies, plantations, rural settlements and *savoka* vegetation seething with reptiles (notably snakes, skinks and colourful chameleons), and a few hours later you will arrive at the park. There are three small, basic but well-managed camps at different altitudes: **Camp Mantella** is in lowland rainforest at 425m (1394ft); **Camp Marojejia** at 750m (2461ft), and above that, accessed by a challenging and steep hike, is **Camp Simpona** (1250m/4101ft). The latter has only eight beds.

Key wildlife in the park includes the endangered all-white silky sifaka, the unmistakeable helmet vanga with its massive blue bill, and a considerable variety of reptiles and frogs, the list of which is still being added to as scientific exploration continues.

Visiting the park is best from late August to end December and it is advisable to be accompanied by experienced guides as the terrain is rugged. Thanks to sterling work by Erik Patel and Eric Mathieu, there is now a growing though small cadre of well-trained and dedicated forest guides who can lead lucky visitors to see the mesmerizing silky sifaka, as well as a large variety of other rainforest wildlife.

Sambava, the access town with the closest airport, can be reached by regular Air Madagascar flights from Antananarivo.

▼ *Below: The silky sifaka is one of the world's rarest and most endangered primates. It can reliably be seen in Marojejy National Park, thanks to intensive work by biologist and lemur expert Erik Patel and his dedicated team of Malagasy conservationists and guides.*

Best Times to Visit

The eastern region receives at least some **rain** on an average of 320 days per anum. Andasibe-Mantadia National Park can be visited all year, but avoid late Jan–Feb due to cyclonic weather. Ste Marie and Pangalanes Canal are pleasant from Apr–Dec. Masoala is at its best from Sep–Dec, with whale-watching Jul–Sep. Visit Marojejy from Sep to early Dec. Climate is hotter on the east coastal plain, with pleasant, warm winters. In the eastern escarpment, winter nights are very cold.

Getting There

The **RN2** road from Tana to Tamatave/Toamasina is in fine condition. Drive time is eight hours or so depending on traffic. From Tana there are daily **flights** to Tamatave/Toamasina and Ste Marie. Regular flights are operated to Maroantsetra, less so to the vanilla centres of Antalaha and Sambava.

Getting Around

Protected sites at Andasibe are a 3-hour drive east of Tana. Continue 80km (50 miles) east to Brickaville (significant as a clash point in the 2002 political crisis) and another 20km (12 miles) to Manambato at Lac Rasoabe, where boats collect guests for hotels on the Pangalanes Canal. A two-hour boat transfer goes to Port Fluvial, Tamatave. Boat transport from Maroantsetra to Masoala and Nosy Mangabe is arranged at hotels in Maroantsetra or lodges in Masoala. Relais du Masoala has the best speedboats. The Sambava–Andapa road is excellent. On Ste Marie, mountain bikes and quad bikes can be hired from some hotels.

Where to Stay

Analamazaotra (Périnet)

LUXURY

Vakona Lodge, tel: 22 6 2480, vakona@ moov.mg www.hotel-vakona.com Ten twin/double rooms and 14 family bungalows, with an additional bedroom on mezzanine. All *en suite*, with heater, mini-bar and safe. On a wooded island are tame lemurs, formerly illegally kept as pets. Horse riding is offered. There is a pool. The lodge is 1km (0.6 miles) from the special reserve entrance. The downside is the 'zoo' including poorly housed fosas.

Andasibe Hote, tel: 034 05 326 27, hotel reception: 034 14 326 27. The best accommodation for visitors to Perinet; 12 comfortable, *en-suite* bungalows: 3 doubles, 3 twins, 1 triple and 3 family bungalows, as well as 2 'VIP villas'. Light, airy design and lovely bathrooms. Situated between Analamazaotra Special Reserve gate and Vakona Forest Lodge, just after the village of Andasibe, 10 minutes' drive from the reserve gate.

MID-RANGE

Eulophiella Lodge, tel: 22 24230 or 032 0756782, www.eulophiella.com Malagasy-owned lodge with 10 standard bungalows and 7 chalets ('Parfums d'Orangers), all widely separated and *en-suite*. Large restaurant with fireplace and terrace. Excellent food and service. Private rainforest reserve where lemurs include diadem sifaka. Great birding. Guided day and night walks. Book in advance; 5km (3 miles) by dirt road off the RN2, it is ideal if you want to escape crowds when Périnet is booked up.

BUDGET

Feon'ny ala, tel: 56 83202. Closest hotel to Analamazaotra. Thirty simple bungalows (21 *en suite*). Lack of heating from April to September is problematic, so pack warm clothing. Overrun with tour groups from Sep–Nov. Food variable.

Pangalanes Canal

MID-RANGE

Bush House, at Akanin'ny Nofy ('nest of dreams'), tel: 22 25878, bushhouse@simicro.mg www.boogiepilgrim-madagascar.com Three nights minimum stay. Owned by Boogie Pilgrim.

MID-RANGE

Le Palmarium, tel: 033 1484 734, hotelpalmarium@yahoo.fr www.palmarium.biz/en Spacious, comfortable bungalows; large rooms have decks with hammock. Good restaurant; relaxed bar. Excellent service. Semi-wild lemurs often visit the restaurant. The 60ha (148-acre) private reserve protects east coast littoral forest. Highly recommended.

Ste Marie (Nosy Boraha)

LUXURY

Princesse Bora Lodge & Spa, tel: 57 0403, mobile: 032

7090 48, www.princesse-bora.com Fifteen villas; comfort bungalows have a suspended double bed; luxury villas are air conditioned, can accommodate two children on the mezzanine level; the glass-fronted executive beach villas can take an extra bed. Three nights minimum stay. Book in advance for whale-watching season (late June to mid-September). The lodge now has an in-house scuba diving centre.

Le Masoandro, tel: 20 23 640 53/4, resa@hsm.mg www.hsm.mg This hotel has 18 bungalows; 'luxe' are more expensive than 'superior'. All are *en suite* and air conditioned. Beautifully located. Infinity pool.

Ile Aux Nattes

MID-RANGE

Baboo Village, tel: 57 04207/032 0479126, infos@baboo-village.com www.baboo-village.com Now the recommended hotel on Ile Aux Nattes, simple, with 14 spacious *en-suite* bungalows, hot water on request. Four are on the ocean. Dining on the jetty. Massages offered; boats and bicycles are available.

Tamatave/Toamasina

LUXURY

Le Neptune, BP 538, Toamasina, tel: 53 32226, Neptune@moov.mg Seaside hotel with 47 rooms overlooking the ocean; pool, restaurant and bar. Disco most nights. Credit cards accepted.

Sharon Hotel, tel: 53 30420, sharonhotel@moov.mg www.sharon-hotel.com Recently renovated, best hotel in town with 44 rooms.

Maroantsetra

LUXURY

Relais du Masoala, tel: 032 40213 81, relaismasoala@gmail.com www.relaisdumasoala.com Fifteen comfortable, *en-suite* bungalows in a 7ha (17-acre) garden with pool. American-owned, award-winning ecolodge. Day and overnight camping excursions to Nosy Mangabe; best speed boat transfers to Masoala National Park; boat trips, birding and whale-watching can be arranged. In October 2012 the proprietor opened the exclusive and beautifully designed Le Petite Relais at Lohatrozona: 8 bungalows near a lovely beach, each with *en-suite* facilities. Good food and excellent service.

Masoala National Park

LUXURY

Masoala Forest Lodge, tel: 22 26114, info@letsgo.ch www.masoalaforestlodge.com Five luxury African safari-styled tents on wooden decks with thatch shelters. Private bathrooms with hot water. Behind the beach at Tampolo Marine Reserve. Activities included in rates are snorkelling, guided rainforest hikes (day and night), sea kayaking, boat trips and visits to the local Betsimisaraka village. Three nights minimum stay required. Open May–Dec.

MID-RANGE

Arol Ecolodge, tel: 033 1290277 or 032 4088902/033 1290277, masoala@free.fr At Lohatrozona rainforest; eight bungalows, three with *en-suite* facilities; five with shared facilities. Excellent food. Simple, small lodge. Cold water. Electricity not available 24/7; solar oven. The lodge assisted Ambodiforaha village by building a school and funds the teacher's salary. The villagers protect a marine reserve (great snorkelling). It's the best location for birders. They arrange treks: Maroantsetra–Arollodge: four days, or Cap Masoala to Arollodge: five days. The most popular package is a night's camping on Nosy Mangabe and two nights at Arollodge.

WHERE TO EAT

All the lodges and hotels mentioned in this section have very good restaurants; most serve continental and Malagasy food.

TAMATAVE	J	F	M	A	M	J	J	A	S	O	N	D
AVERAGE TEMP. °C	30	30	30	30	27	25	25	25	30	32	32	33
AVERAGE TEMP. °F	86	86	86	86	81	77	77	77	86	90	39	90
RAINFALL mm	413	382	479	323	228	259	285	218	121	133	169	357
RAINFALL in	16.3	15.1	18.9	12.7	9	10.2	11.2	8.6	4.8	5.2	6.7	14.1
DAYS OF RAINFALL	22	26	20	15	14	12	10	13	12	10	16	19

Travel Tips

Tourist Information

See relevant At A Glance section in each chapter.

Embassies Abroad

USA: 2374 Massachussets Avenue, Washington DC., 20008 USA, tel: 202 265 5525/26/27, fax: 202 265 3034 or 202 483 7603, e-mail: Malagasy.embassy@verison.net
Canada: 03 Raymond Street, Ottawa, Ontario K1R 1A3, tel: 613 567 0505, fax: 613 567 2882, e-mail: ambamadcanada@bellnet.ca website: www.madagascar-embassy.ca
South Africa: 90 B Tait Street, Colbyn, Pretoria 0002, P O Box 11722, Queenswood 0121, Pretoria, tel: 27 12 342 0983/4/5, fax: 27 12 342 0995, e-mail: ambamad.pta@infodoor.co.za
Australia: Level 4, 47 York Street, Sydney, NSW 2000. tel: 61 02 9299 2290, fax: 61 02 9299 2242, e-mail: consul@madagascarconsulate.com.au
France: 4 Avenue Raphael, 75016 Paris, tel: 01 45 04 62 11, fax: 01 45 03 58 70 e-mail: info@ambassade-madagascar.fr website: www.ambassade-madagascar.fr

Entry Requirements

Your passport must be valid for at least six months beyond your intended visit. It must contain at least one blank page for the entry visa or you may be denied entry. British, other EU, American, Canadian, South African and Australian passport holders require a visa for entry to Madagascar. Visas may be issued by a Malagasy embassy, or on arrival at Ivato or Nosy Bé airports. Visa forms are in the *Passeport pour Madagascar* booklet, distributed on all international flights. A one-month, single-entry visa is issued on arrival and at the time of writing is free (Jan 2013). Allow up to an hour for immigration formalities.

Getting There

See relevant At A Glance section in each chapter.

Travel Insurance

It is essential that you have comprehensive travel insurance. Some credit card companies provide travel insurance if you pay for your holiday by credit card. Check the extent of cover provided with your card company – it may not be adequate. You should arrange separate insurance cover for valuable items before you go. Leave expensive jewellery at home.

Documents

Take a certified copy of your insurance policy with you. Leave this document, certified copies of your passports and a note of the numbers of any travellers' cheques with a reliable contact at home, in case originals are lost or stolen. Take an additional certified photocopy of your passport and of your airline tickets with you and leave copies at home.

Mobile Phones

With international roaming it is possible to take your mobile phone with you and signal is available in most of the larger urban centres, and near some parks. Taking a mobile phone with a battery charger is a wise idea, should anything go wrong during your trip.

Health Requirements

There are no compulsory health requirements at present, unless you are arriving from East Africa, in which case a yellow fever certificate is required, or you will be vaccinated at the airport ... not a pleasant thought.
There is a risk of malaria and precautions, including anti-malaria tablets and insect repellent, are imperative. Some strains of malaria are resistant to certain prophylactics and you are advised to take precautions (i.e. insect repellent, long trousers). Pack wet-wipes and use them after handling currency to reduce the risk of digestive upsets. (Grubby local currency has been known to carry bacteria, including salmonella.)
Never drink unpurified water. Bottled water is available almost everywhere. People planning camping trips should take water purification tablets with them.
Avoid ice cream and yoghurt. Peel fruit before eating it. Pack medication for digestive upsets, headaches, pain relief and respiratory conditions and take plasters and antiseptic creams along. Take jelly-shoes or flip-flops to protect your feet against sea urchins, which are abundant in some parts of the country's shallow seas.
The strong African sun can cause severe burns and sunstroke in a few hours. Pack the necessary precautions (light clothing, hat, sunglasses and sun block). AIDS is widespread. Your physician is the best source of accurate information on health requirements. Avoid dogs, cats and do not try to hold onto tame lemurs – they are still wild animals.
Immunization against rabies is not a requirement, though some view it as 'immunization against worry'.

Health Clinics:
UK: Hospital for Tropical Diseases Travel Clinic, Mortimer Market Building, Capper Street, Tottenham Court Road, London WC1E 6JB, tel: 02 07 3889600, www.thehtd.org Opening hours: Wednesdays 13:00–17:00; Fridays from 09:00–13:00 only.
MASTA (tel: 0870 6062782, www.masta-travel-health.com) offers flexible appointments at short notice, particularly for people who need vaccinations close to departure dates.
USA: Centre for Disease Control, tel: 800 3113435, www.cdc.gov/travel
Australia and New Zealand: IAMAT, www.iamat.org
South Africa:
SAA-Netcare Travel Clinics, www.travelclinic.co.za

Tour Operators

The most practical manner in which to arrange a hassle-free trip, is to contact a reputable Madagascar-specialist tour operator. This means you could benefit from low-cost airfares, and you have control over your itinerary. You will receive advice as to which places are suitable (or unsuitable) for travel during the time/s you have available and save enormously on wasting precious time in a remote country which you may visit but once. Internationally, the top three Madagascar specialists are:
USA: Cortez Travel, Inc., tel: 619 755 5136, e-mail: info@cortez-usa.com website: www.cortez-usa.com
UK: Rainbow Tours, tel: 0207 666 1250, e-mail: info@rainbowtours.co.uk website: www.rainbowtours.co.uk
South Africa: Jenman Safaris, tel: 021 683 7826, e-mail: info@jenmansafaris.com website: www.jenmansafaris.com

Air Travel

Check in early for both international and domestic flights. Allow a minimum of three hours for international and two hours for domestic flights. Airlines can overbook so the earlier you check in, the less likely you are to experience problems. Once in Madagascar, reconfirm onward flight reservations at least 72 hours prior to your departure.
Always pack luggage so you have essential items for the first three days in your hand luggage: bags can go astray

and may only arrive in Madagascar three or four days later. In the event that your luggage has gone missing or was damaged, report it immediately to the airline representative in the baggage reclaim area. Complete a Property Irregularity Report and keep a copy for your travel insurance company.

What to Pack

Lightweight, long clothing (long-sleeved shirts and long trousers/slacks). T-shirts and shorts/skirts. Warm trousers, jersey/sweater and fleece for evenings in montane rainforests. Day bag/sack. Good walking shoes or hiking boots for steep trails. Raincoats and small umbrella for rainforest reserves. Thongs/flip-flops/jelly-shoes to protect your feet from coral and sea urchins. Hat with wide brim or peak with neck-flap. Good quality sunglasses. Spare pair of spectacles if you wear contact lenses. Insect repellent. Personal toiletries and medication. Tickets, passport, insurance documents and money. Camera equipment, batteries (and film). Binoculars. Strong torch/flashlight and spare batteries. Wet wipes or instant hand cleanser. Snorkelling equipment (masks only). Beach towel/mat (provided at upscale beach resorts). Towel and toilet roll for camping. Malaria prophylactic tablets and medical supplies. Water bottle. Course of broad-spectrum antibiotic. For wildlife hot spots, take camera, binoculars (large 8x40 is useful), sun hat, sun block and insect repellent. If visiting a rainforest, pack a waterproof jacket and comfortable shoes. If you are camping, take warm clothing, a towel and soap, antiseptic wipes and a roll of toilet paper. Plastic bags, especially for wet walking shoes if travelling on a busy itinerary.

Business Hours

Generally **office hours** are 08:00–12:00 and 14:00–17:00. **Banks** are open Monday to Friday from 08:00–16:00 and close the afternoon before public holidays. **Hotel check-in:** Usually bedrooms are available from 14:00. Check-out is mostly expected by 11:00. Some hotels provide rest areas and storage facilities. If you need earlier access to a room, make a reservation for the previous night, or for day use. Notify hotels or tour operators if early breakfasts are required.

Camping

Note carefully: other than in designated camp sites in protected areas, camping is sometimes frowned on in Madagascar. It is permitted along river routes, such as the Tsiribihina or Manambolo – in which case tourists would be accompanied by a local guide, who is able to assist in terms of translation, facilitating, and ascertaining the nature of local *fady*. Camp sites are mostly in demarcated areas, but rudimentary and with limited or no facilities at all. (Some such as Ranomafana and Ankarafantsika have tent shelters and platforms, and communal facilities.)

Communications

From the outside world to Madagascar, and within Madagascar, communications are still a tedious process, though there has been improvement. The international dialling code for Madagascar is +261 20. For land-line numbers, dial +261-20 + city/town code + number. For mobile/cellphone numbers replace 20

Conversion Chart

From	To	Multiply By
Millimetres	Inches	0.0394
Metres	Yards	1.0936
Metres	Feet	3.281
Kilometres	Miles	0.6214
Square kilometres	Square miles	0.386
Hectares	Acres	2.471
Litres	Pints	1.760
Kilograms	Pounds	2.205
Tonnes	Tons	0.984

To convert Celsius to Fahrenheit: x 9 ÷ 5 + 32

with 32 or 33. **Antananarivo:** 22 or 24; **Antsirabe:** 44; **Antsirañana/Diégo Suarez:** 82; **Fianarantsoa:** 75; **Mahajanga:** 62; **Morondava:** 95; **Nosy Bé:** 86; **Sambava:** 88; **Tôlañaro/Fort Dauphin:** 92; **Toamasina/Tamatave:** 53; **Toliara/Tuléar:** 94.
You can buy phone cards, which allow for cheaper calls from land-lines.
Cellphones/Mobile phones: If you take your own and arrange international roaming facilities, you should have cover in larger urban centres, but usually not in national parks. You can also buy pre-paid sim cards in Tana.
Internet: In the larger urban centres there are now many cyber-cafés, but the majority have French keyboards. Connection can be slow. Many hotels have Internet access.

Transport

For car hire information, *see* page 83. **Roads:** The achievements of the Ravalomanana government with regard to upgrading the national road system was remarkable. The main roads linking large ports to the capital (Toamasina, Tuléar, Mahajanga) are in excellent shape. Some rural roads may be appalling. Drivers require an international license. Taxis do not have meters so agree on a fare before setting out.
Railways: At time of writing the only route functional for passengers is that from Fianarantsoa to Manakara. This may change in the next year or two.

Money Matters

Currency: The local currency is the Malagasy Ariary (MGA). Ariary notes have a metallic strip on the right-hand side. In January 2013, GBP = 3,658 MGA, US$1 = 2,251 MGA, 1 euro = 2,970 MGA.
While there are exchange facilities in the main cities during the working week, service may be restricted to certain hours. Changing money can be lengthy and frustrating.
An unlimited amount of travellers' cheques may be taken into Madagascar, provided you present the receipt for purchase of the cheques. However, changing of travellers cheques is increasingly difficult (at time of writing, almost impossible), so rather take cash.
A maximum of 400,000 Ariary may be taken out of Madagascar. Failure to observe this prohibition will result in confiscation of the Malagasy money.
Cash: Take euros or US$. Large-denomination dollar/euro bank notes are not generally accepted because of counterfeit activities. Ask for some small denomination notes (Ar.100 and Ar. 200) for tips and local purchases.
The amount of spending money varies individually. In smarter hotels, a good three-course meal costs up to £20 per person; a bottle of local wine about £4–£5 and a bottle of mineral water about £1.50 in a bar and 80p in a shop or *hotely*. Please note that, in the airport departure lounge, you will need hard currency.

Public Holidays

1 January • New Year's Day
29 March • National Day
Late March/early April • Good Friday and Easter Monday
Late April/May • Ascension
1 May • Labour Day
Late May/early June • Whitsun Monday
26 June • Independence Day
15 August • Assumption Day
1 November • All Saints' Day
25 December • Christmas Day
30 December • Republic Day

Credit Cards: While Visa and American Express are increasingly useful in Madagascar, they are not accepted by all hotels, and usually not by restaurants or shops. Where cards are accepted, the transaction fee is often between 3 and 8%. Do not rely on cards for obtaining local currency from the bank at the airport. Cards can, however, sometimes be useful for drawing cash from banks in the main towns. Except for in Maroantsetra, Mastercard is handled by few banks in Madagascar and generally cannot be used to purchase goods and services.
Tipping: Here are some guidelines (January 2013): Guides: Ar. 10,000 per person per day; drivers: Ar. 5000 per person per day; forest/reserve guides, whose employment varies seasonally: Ar. 15,000 per person per day; hotel staff (porters and bellhops): Ar. 1000 per item of luggage.

The service charge in restaurants is usually 10%, at your discretion. Where there is a tipping box for the hotel or lodge staff, you could leave Ar. 10,000 per person per day. This should be equitably distributed among staff.

Local Time

GMT plus three hours.

Electricity

220V, European two-prong plugs.

Weights and Measures

Madagascar uses the metric system.

Language

Malagasy is the first language. French is the business language. The use of English is increasing in hotels.

Health Precautions

Most cities and towns have well-stocked pharmacies. *See* relevant At A Glance section. **Private clinics** in Antananarivo, Medical Plus, tel: 22 56758. 24-hour home/hotel visits and ambulance service.

Safety

Theft occurs in larger urban centres, especially Tana. Wear a money belt. Leave valuables with hotel reception. Use a combination lock on luggage.

Swimming: Avoid swimming along the east coast of Madagascar – sharks are a danger from Fort Dauphin to Diégo Suarez. Swimming is safe along the reef-protected west side of Ile Sainte Marie and where local guides advise off Masoala. Swimming is mostly safe off Nosy Bé, Anjajavy, Morondava and the southwest coast. Do not swim in the sea if you have an open wound or are menstruating.

Scuba Diving: Divers need to be experienced, not just recently qualified. Madagascar has no hyperbaric chamber so casualties must be evacuated to Réunion, Kenya, South Africa or Mauritius, where there are recompression facilities. *See* the website of Divers Alert Network for details of evacuation insurance: www.diversalertnetwork.org Be sure the dive operator you are diving with has oxygen supplies on the boat.

Etiquette

Tourists or *vazaha* are often exempt from adhering to *fady*, the complex system of beliefs that operates in Madagascar. But the degree of tolerance varies, and it is wise and considerate to find out which customs apply. Your guides are the best people to inform you of the local customs and beliefs. The cult of ancestors and Christianity are at the centre of Malagasy culture. Tombs are the sacred dwellings of the ancestors. Refrain from pointing at them. When visiting sacred spots, ask your guide whether photography is permitted. Always ask people if you may photograph them. Sometimes they will agree in exchange for a gift or some money. Do not take photographs around government buildings or military bases. People appreciate being greeted in Malagasy. Shaking hands is custom. Public demonstrations of affection are not considered appropriate.

Off the beaten track: Communities are governed by a council of elders or *fokonolona*. If you are in a remote rural site and in need of accommodation, always ask permission from the local *President du Fokontany*. At times a hut or house may be kept for visitors, or vacated when visitors arrive. It is considered offensive to refuse such hospitality. Often the most unexpectedly wonderful meals are served. A small but reasonable payment to your host or hostess is expected.

Good Reading

- **Goodman, S, et al**, *The Natural History of Madagascar* (University Of Chicago Press, 2nd edition, 2007)
- **Langrand, O** and **Sinclair, I**, *Field Guide to the Birds of the Indian Ocean Islands* (Struik/New Holland, 2nd edition 2006)
- **Mittermeier, R, et al**, *Conservation International: Lemurs of Madagascar*; (Tropical Field Guide Series, 3rd edition 2011)
- **Bradt, H, Schuurman, D, and Garbutt, N,** *Madagascar Wildlife: A Visitors Guide* (Bradt, UK, 3rd edition 2008)

INDEX

Note: Numbers in **bold** indicate photographs

Africa 5, 6, 8, 16
Akanin'ny Nofy 110
Akany Avoko 40
Alley of Giant Baobabs **71**, 77
aloes 10, 54, 89
Ambalavao 35, 37, 44–45
Ambanja 88, 97
Ambataloaka 89, **94**
Ambodifotatra **112**, 113
Ambohimanga 40
Ambositra 42
Ampijoroa (Ankarafantsika) 72, **73**, 74, 83
Anakao 10, 51, 52, 53, 55–56
Analakely Market 38
Analamazaotra Forest Station 103, 104, 105
Andapa 119,
Andrianampoinimerina, King 16, 39
Anjaha Community Conservation Site 45
Anjajavy 75
Anjozorobe 41
Ankarana Special Reserve 87, 91–93
Antananarivo 9, 17, 23, 27, **37**, 38–40
Antongil Bay 112, 115, 116, 117
Antsirabe 27, 37, 41, 42
Appert's greenbul 56
Arboretum de Antsokay 53
Artisans' Market **26**, 38
asity
Schlegel's 74
common sunbird 44, 105
velvet 44
Association Mitsinjo 106
Avenue de l'Indépendance 38
aye aye 10, 11, 40, 116, 117

Baie des Dunes 89
Baie des Forbans 113
Baie des Sakalavas 89
Baie de Sainte-Luce 61, **62**
baobab 6, 8, 10, 54, 55, 63, **71**, 72, 75, 77, 78, 83, 87, 90
Baobab Centre 81
bats 10, 11, 64, 77, 92, 108
Bekopaka 78, 82
Belo-Sur-Mer 79, 83
Belo Sur Tsiribihina 7, 81, 82
Bemaraha plateau 7, 10, 77
Bernier's vanga 118
Betsiboka River 21
boa constrictors **40**, 41, 64
bone-turning ceremony **29**
Boothby, Richard 55
Bush House 110
Bush, Paddy 32

Cameron, James 39
Cascade Grande **90**
Centre Fihavanana 28, 40
Chez Chabaud 74
Classic Camping, Madagascar 66
climate 8
Cirque Rouge 75
common tenrec 11, 44, 64, 92
Coton de Tuléar 63
Coua:
blue 105
Coquerel's 74, 76
crested 56, 79, 93
giant 56, 64
red-fronted 105
red-capped 80
Crocodile Caves (Ankarana) 87
cyclones 8, 27, 103, 105

deciduous dry forests **10**, 71, **73**, 80, 82
Dias, Diego 16, 17, 88
Diégo Suarez 8, 28, 87, 88–89
Drury, Robert 57
Durrell Wildlife Conservation Trust 11, 73, 76, 109

eastern avahi 44, 105
equitrade 97
euphorbia-didieraceae bush **53**
Evatraha 61
Exorcism (toby) 58

fady 31, 56, 76, 83, 110, 116
famadihana 19, 27, **29**
FANAMBY 74, 77
Fianarantsoa 23, 28, 35, 37, 41, 43, 44
fihavanana 27
Fort Dauphin 26, 51, 53, 58, 59, 60, **61**, 62
fosa 11, 13, **56**, 78, 92
fringed gecko (Uroplatus) 37, 74, **115**, 116
frogs 10, 13, 40, 58, 61, 76, 81, 96, 105, 106, 117
giant jumping rat 11, 13, 76, 78
giant hog-nosed snake 13, 74
Gondwana 5, 6, 10
green day-gecko (Phelsuma) 12
Grotte d'Andrafiabe 92

Haute-Ville
Antananarivo 39
Fianarantsoa 43
Hauts Plateaux 6
helicopter trips 30
Hell-Ville 89, 94, 95, 97
Horombe plateau **6**, 46
humpback whales 114, 117, 112

Ifaty 10, 46, 51, 52, 54–55
Ifotaka Community Forest 66
Ihosy 46
Ile Aux Nattes 103, 113, 114
Ile Sainte Marie 103
IMF (International Monetary Fund) 16, 25
Indian Ocean 8, 17, 18, 112, 115
indri 10, **11**, 104, 105, 108
Isalo 46, 52, **57–59**
Ivato International Airport 16, 38

Joffreville 88, 89, 92
Jolly, Lady Alison 26, 63

kabosy 33
Katsepy 74
Kidd, William 112, 115
kiloloka 33
Kirindy 13, 71, 77, 78–80

La Table 55
Laborde, Jean 19, 20, 35, 39, 40
Lakes (Lac)
Alaotra 103, 107, 109
Anosy **37**, 39
Mantasoa 40–41
Ravelobe 73, 74
Tsimanampetsotsa 51, 56
Vert **92**
lamba 33
language 17, 28, 30, 33
Langrand, Olivier 81
leaf-tailed gecko 41, 44, 74, 90, 106
lemur
Alaotra reed 11, 109
aye aye 10, 11, 40, 116, 117
black **4**, 11, 96, 97
lemur (cont.)
black-and-white ruffed 43, 107, 112, 116
brown 43, 56, 64, 73, 75, 105, 108
Cleese's woolly 81
collared brown 61, 64
Coquerel's giant mouse 78
Coquerel's sifaka 73, 75
crowned 90, 92, **93**
crowned sifaka 74
eastern lesser (grey) bamboo 43
fork-marked 78, 91, 117
golden bamboo 14, 43
golden-brown mouse 73
golden-crowned sifaka 74
Goodman's mouse 105
greater bamboo 14, 106
greater dwarf 44
grey-backed sportive 96
indri 10, **11**, 104, 105, 106, 108
Madame Berthe's mouse 10, 79
Milne-Edwards' diadem sifaka 42, 43, 107, 108
Milne-Edwards' sportive 73
mongoose 73, 74
northern mouse 92
pygmy mouse **79**, 81
red-bellied 43,112
red-fronted brown 43, 64, 78, 81
red-ruffed 11
ring-tailed 11, 37, 45, 56, 62, 64, **66**
rufous mouse 44
small-toothed sportive 44
southern lesser bamboo 65
Verreaux's sifaka **56**, 64, 65, 78
western grey bamboo 81
white-footed sportive 64
white-fronted 112, 116
Local guides 62, 110
Lohatrozona 117
Lokaro 61
Lokobe 96
London Missionary Society 18, 20, 21

Madacraft 24
Madagascar
crested ibis 90,
fish eagle 74, 76, 79, 81, **83**, 98
nightjar 58
partridge 56
plover 56
pochard 107

INDEX

Madagascar (cont.)
red owl 118
serpent eagle 118
Madagascar Classic Camping 66
MAP 24, 110
Madagascar Fauna Group 40, 112
Mahafaly tomb 15, 30, 52, 53
Mahajanga 7, 21, 27, 71–72, 74
Manambolo River 7, 78
Manda Beach **111**
Mandena Conservation Site 61
Mandrare River **6**, 52, 62
Mangoky River 7
Mantadia-Vohidrazana rainforest block 104
Marais de Torotorofotsy 104, 106
Maroantsetra 8, 111, **114**, 115
Marodoka 94
Maromizaha rainforest 104
Masoala
National Park 103, 115, 116–118
Peninsula 9, 80, 114, **117**
Rainforest 13, **116**
MATE (Man And The Environment) 107
MEGAPTERA (whale-watching) 112
Meier, Bernard 14, 43
mesite
brown 44
sub-desert 54
white-breasted 74, 93
Miandrivaso town 78, 82
missionaries 16, 18, 20
Mitsio Islands 79, 87, 95, 97–98
Montagne d'Ambre 9, 11, 87, 89, 91
Montagne des Français 88–89
montane rainforest 9, **13**, 41, 104
Moramanga 103, **108**
Morondava 7, 8, 71, 77, 78, 81, 82
Mount Maromokotro 6, 87
Mozambique Channel 8, 82
Musée Mahafaly-Sakalava 53

Nahampoahana Wildlife Sanctuary 62
Namorona River 43
national parks and reserves
Analamazaotra Special Reserve 104–105
national parks and reserves (cont.)
Andasibe-Mantadia National Park 11, 103–104
Andohahela National Park 65–66
Andringitra National Park 45–46
Anjajavy Reserve 75–77
Ankarafantsika National Park 11, 71, 72–74
Ankarana Special Reserve 87, 91–93
Berenty Private Reserve 52, 60, 62–64
Betampona Reserve 112
Ialatsara Lemur Park 42
Isalo National Park 51, **57**–59
Lac Tsimanampetsotsa National Park 51, 56
Lokobe Reserve 96
Mantadia National Park 106–107
Marojejy National Park 103, 118–119
Masoala National Park 103, 116
Montagne d'Ambre National Park 87, 89–91
Nahampoahana Wildlife Sanctuary 62
Nosy Mangabe Reserve 115–116
Ranomafana National Park **13**, 14, 37, 43–44
Tsingy de Bemaraha National Park 71, 78, 80–82
Zombitse-Vohibasia National Park 8, 56
night walks 13, 41, 44, 64, 76, 80, 91, 104, 108
Nosy (island)
Bé 19, 33, 72, 77, **87**, 89, 93, **94**, 95, 96
Boraha 112–114
Komba 95, 97
Lonja **89**
Mangabe 10, 13, 115–116
Saba 98
Tanikely 93, 96–97
Tsarabanjina 6
Vé 51, 55, 56

Onilahy River 57
orchids **9**, 44, 56, 61, 114, 118
Oustalet's chameleon 12, 76, 79
pachypodium 10, 54, **59**, 65, 81
Pangalanes Canal 7, **102**, 103, 108, **109**–110
Parc Ivoloina 112
Périnet 9, 11, **104**, 107
Pic Imarivolanitra ('Boby') 45
pirates' cemetery 15, 113
Piscine Naturelle 57
pitcher plants **63**, 110
pitta-like ground-roller 44, 107
ploughshare tortoise **74**
prickly pear cactus (*raketa*) 63

Ramena Beach 89
Ranohira 46, 57, 59
Ranomafana *see* national parks and reserves
Rakotozafy (musician) 109
Ratsiraka, Didier 16, 21, 22
Ravalomanana, Marc 15, 16, 23, 24
ReefDoctor 54
Razamanasy, Guy 16, 22
rice paddies 37, 78, 119
ring-tailed mongoose **44**, 92
river trips 78
Rova **18**, **19**, 39
ruiniforme sandstone formations **57**

Sakaraha 53, 57
Salary Bay 55
Sambava 118, 119
Sarodrano Cave 55
Sickle-billed vanga **12**, 93
silky sifaka **119**
Silver Palace 39
sorcerers 31, 32
spiny bush 9, 51, 52, 54, 55, 59, 63, 65, 66
spiny desert 46, **53**
St Augustin Bay 55
Ste Marie 17, **20**, **103**, 112–114
striped civet 44, 92
stump-tailed chameleons (Brookesia) 12

Tamatave (Toamasina) 7, 27, 103, 109, **111**–112
Tampolo Marine Reserve 117
taxi-brousse **82**
tea 44
tenrec 11, 31, 44, 64, 92, 117, **119**
tomato frog **117**
tribes
Antaifasy 29
Antaisaka 29, 31
tribes (cont.)
Antakarana 19, 29, 88
Antamboahaka 29
Antandroy 15, 29, **32**, 46, 51, 52, 53, 59, 63, 66
Antanosy 17, 29, 53, 59, 60, 61
Bara 29, 46, 57
Betsileo 17, 18, 29, 31, 33, 43
Betsimisaraka 18, 19, 29, 103
Bezanozano 29, 103
Boina Sakalava 18, 19, 29, **33**
Mahafaly 15, 29, 53, 59
Masikoro 29, 52
Merina 16, 17–18, 29, 37, 38
Sakalava 15, 17, 29, 31, 56, 63, 71, 75, 76, 79, 94
Sihanaka 29, 103, 109
Tanala 29
Tsimehety 29
Veso 46, 52, 54, 55, 71, 83
Tritriva volcanic lake 42
tromba 75
Tsaratanana massif 87
Tsimbazaza
Botanical Gardens 40
Museum 40
Zoo 40
tsingy 7, 71, 77, 80, **81**, 87, **91**
tsiny 114
Tuléar 8, 41, 42, 51, 52–53
turtles
green 93
hawksbill 93
loggerhead 93

vakana 28, **34**
Vali, Justin 32,33
Valiha 32,33
Varavarana ny Atsimo 46
Vohimana 104, **107**–108

white-browed owl 58, 64
white-throated oxylabes 90
white-throated rail 58
Wilmé, Lucienne 44, 106, 107
World Bank 14, 16, 25
Worldwide Fund for Nature (WWF) 14, 54, 56
Wright, Patricia 14, 26, 43

Zafy, Albert 16, 22
zebu
cattle 14, 23, 31
ox carts 46, 59